Number 149
Spring 2016

New Directions for Evaluation

Paul R. Brandon
Editor-in-Chief

Evaluation and Facilitation

Rita Sinorita Fierro
Alissa Schwartz
Dawn Hanson Smart
Editors

EVALUATION AND FACILITATION
Rita Sinorita Fierro, Alissa Schwartz, Dawn Hanson Smart (eds.)
New Directions for Evaluation, no. 149
Paul R. Brandon, Editor-in-Chief

Microfilm copies of issues and articles are available in 16mm and 35mm, as well as microfiche in 105mm, through University Microfilms Inc., 300 North Zeeb Road, Ann Arbor, MI 48106-1346.

New Directions for Evaluation is indexed in Academic Search Alumni Edition (EBSCO Publishing), Education Research Complete (EBSCO Publishing), Higher Education Abstracts (Claremont Graduate University), SCOPUS (Elsevier), Social Services Abstracts (ProQuest), Sociological Abstracts (ProQuest), Worldwide Political Science Abstracts (ProQuest).

NEW DIRECTIONS FOR EVALUATION (ISSN 1097-6736, electronic ISSN 1534-875X) is part of The Jossey-Bass Education Series and is published quarterly by Wiley Subscription Services, Inc., A Wiley Company, at Jossey-Bass, One Montgomery Street, Suite 1200, San Francisco, CA 94104-4594.

SUBSCRIPTIONS for individuals cost $89 for U.S./Canada/Mexico/international. For institutions, $358 U.S.; $398 Canada/Mexico; $432 international. Electronic only: $89 for individuals all regions; $358 for institutions all regions. Print and electronic: $98 for individuals in the U.S., Canada, and Mexico; $122 for individuals for the rest of the world; $430 for institutions in the U.S.; $470 for institutions in Canada and Mexico; $504 for institutions for the rest of the world.

All issues are proposed by guest editors. For proposal submission guidelines, go to http://www.eval.org/p/cm/ld/fid=48. Editorial correspondence should be addressed to the Editor-in-Chief, Paul R. Brandon, University of Hawai'i at Mānoa, 1776 University Avenue, Castle Memorial Hall Rm 118, Honolulu, HI 96822-2463.

www.josseybass.com

Cover photograph by ©iStock.com/Smithore

New Directions for Evaluation

Sponsored by the American Evaluation Association

EDITOR-IN-CHIEF

Paul R. Brandon	University of Hawai'i at Mānoa

ASSOCIATE EDITORS

J. Bradley Cousins	University of Ottawa
Lois-ellin Datta	Datta Analysis

EDITORIAL ADVISORY BOARD

Anna Ah Sam	University of Hawai'i at Mānoa
Michael Bamberger	Independent consultant
Gail Barrington	Barrington Research Group, Inc.
Fred Carden	International Development Research Centre
Thomas Chapel	Centers for Disease Control and Prevention
Leslie Cooksy	Sierra Health Foundation
Fiona Cram	Katoa Ltd.
Peter Dahler-Larsen	University of Southern Denmark
E. Jane Davidson	Real Evaluation Ltd.
Stewart Donaldson	Claremont Graduate University
Jody Fitzpatrick	University of Colorado Denver
Jennifer Greene	University of Illinois at Urbana-Champaign
Melvin Hall	Northern Arizona University
George M. Harrison	University of Hawai'i at Mānoa
Gary Henry	Vanderbilt University
Rodney Hopson	George Mason University
George Julnes	University of Baltimore
Jean King	University of Minnesota
Saville Kushner	University of Auckland
Robert Lahey	REL Solutions Inc.
Miri Levin-Rozalis	Ben Gurion University of the Negev and Davidson Institute at the Weizmann Institute of Science
Laura Leviton	Robert Wood Johnson Foundation
Melvin Mark	Pennsylvania State University
Sandra Mathison	University of British Columbia
Robin Lin Miller	Michigan State University
Michael Morris	University of New Haven
Debra Rog	Westat and the Rockville Institute
Patricia Rogers	Royal Melbourne Institute of Technology
Mary Ann Scheirer	Scheirer Consulting
Robert Schwarz	University of Toronto
Lyn Shulha	Queen's University
Nick L. Smith	Syracuse University
Sanjeev Sridharan	University of Toronto
Monica Stitt-Bergh	University of Hawai'i at Mānoa

Editorial Policy and Procedures

New Directions for Evaluation, a quarterly sourcebook, is an official publication of the American Evaluation Association. The journal publishes works on all aspects of evaluation, with an emphasis on presenting timely and thoughtful reflections on leading-edge issues of evaluation theory, practice, methods, the profession, and the organizational, cultural, and societal context within which evaluation occurs. Each issue of the journal is devoted to a single topic, with contributions solicited, organized, reviewed, and edited by one or more guest editors.

The editor-in-chief is seeking proposals for journal issues from around the globe about topics new to the journal (although topics discussed in the past can be revisited). A diversity of perspectives and creative bridges between evaluation and other disciplines, as well as chapters reporting original empirical research on evaluation, are encouraged. A wide range of topics and substantive domains are appropriate for publication, including evaluative endeavors other than program evaluation; however, the proposed topic must be of interest to a broad evaluation audience.

Journal issues may take any of several forms. Typically they are presented as a series of related chapters, but they might also be presented as a debate; an account, with critique and commentary, of an exemplary evaluation; a feature-length article followed by brief critical commentaries; or perhaps another form proposed by guest editors.

Submitted proposals must follow the format found via the Association's website at http://www.eval.org/Publications/NDE.asp. Proposals are sent to members of the journal's Editorial Advisory Board and to relevant substantive experts for single-blind peer review. The process may result in acceptance, a recommendation to revise and resubmit, or rejection. The journal does not consider or publish unsolicited single manuscripts.

Before submitting proposals, all parties are asked to contact the editor-in-chief, who is committed to working constructively with potential guest editors to help them develop acceptable proposals. For additional information about the journal, see the "Statement of the Editor-in-Chief" in the Spring 2013 issue (No. 137).

Paul R. Brandon, Editor-in-Chief
University of Hawai'i at Mānoa
College of Education
1776 University Avenue
Castle Memorial Hall, Rm. 118
Honolulu, HI 968222463
e-mail: nde@eval.org

Contents

Editors' Notes

There are many intersections between evaluation and facilitation. The profession of evaluation is about applying systematic methods to gain knowledge, but it can focus on basic inquiry and investigation, monitoring and accountability, program improvement, and organizational learning, as well. The profession of facilitation focuses on work with groups, but again with a breadth of purposes from information and idea exchange to knowledge development, decision making, problem solving, conflict resolution, and team building. This issue explores the interplay between evaluation and facilitation, how one practice can inform and serve the other.

Many evaluation steps are undertaken with groups and require evaluators to play a facilitative role—to engage stakeholders in meaningful conversation, to structure these discussions in ways that surface multiple perspectives, and to conduct focus groups on key data and make progress toward next steps or decision making. Facilitation can help groups map theories of change, undertake data collection through focus groups or other dialogues, participate in analysis of findings, and craft appropriate recommendations based on these findings. In each step, an evaluator must be cognizant of the interactions and power dynamics among group members, help differences of opinion emerge while finding common ground, and manage disparate agendas and conflicts. While each of these steps is explained in evaluation textbooks and publications and attention is given to describing facilitation approaches and techniques, how these approaches and techniques are applied and adapted in different situations and the skills and competencies needed to master them are not extensively discussed or well documented.

In facilitation there are similar process steps—planning individual or multiple sessions, conducting those meetings, adjusting the plan in the moment, following up on the interactions and meeting content, and assessing the progress or results accomplished. A great deal of information is available about facilitative approaches and techniques, and while evaluating the process and outcome of the work is seen as critical to learning and helping groups make progress, little about purposeful evaluation of facilitation is published.

The Literature

The disciplines of evaluation and facilitation are different, but there are overlaps in the theories that underlie them. *Social interdependence* theory (see Deutsch, 1949a, 1949b, 1973, 2006; D. W. Johnson & F. P. Johnson, 2009; D. W. Johnson & R. T. Johnson, 1989, 2005; D. W. Johnson, Johnson,

NEW DIRECTIONS FOR EVALUATION, no. 149, Spring 2016   © 2016 Wiley Periodicals, Inc., and the American Evaluation Association.   Published online in Wiley Online Library (wileyonlinelibrary.com) • DOI: 10.1002/ev.20175

& Stevahn, 2011) provides one foundation for both evaluators and facilitators, describing how cooperative relationships among those involved in a process are more likely to result in interactions that benefit everyone. Research on evaluation use (see Alkin, Daillak, & White, 1979; Brandon & Singh, 2009; Cousins & Leithwood, 1986; K. Johnson et al., 2009; King & Pechman, 1984; Kirkhart, 2000; Ottoson & Martinez, 2010; Patton, 2008, 2012; Preskill & Caracelli, 1997; Shula & Cousins, 1997; Weiss, 1972, 1998) provides another supporting base, demonstrating the benefits of engaging and involving stakeholders in the development of shared meaning, deeper learning, and the use of evaluation results for decision making and quality improvement. *Organizational theory* is a third, with a broad base of literature related to learning and adaptation within organizations and how it takes place. The literature here is comprehensively summarized by Fiol and Lyles (1985) and Scott (2011). Among the most referenced theorists are Easterby-Smith, Crossan, and Nicolini (2000), Huber (1991), Lewin (1947, 1953), and Weick and Westley (1996).

Evaluation and facilitation share the desire to "enable reflection" and "foster learning." These elements are integral to moving forward, whether this means moving ahead to a next step in a multistep process or toward decisions that lead to improvements or problem solving, organizational change, or sustainability development.

Facilitation, as a part of evaluation work, is not a new concept, given the development and growing usage of participatory and empowerment evaluation and action research. Many articles in *New Directions in Evaluation* address participatory evaluation. An issue from the late 90s, *Understanding and Practicing Participatory Evaluation* (1998), and the more specialized issue *Youth Participatory Evaluation* (2003), provide a solid foundation. Both talk about facilitation as part of the process and relevant issues such as power sharing, objectivity, and competency in facilitation skills. Neither discusses how to evaluate facilitation and its impact on the evaluation process. Other NDE issues include articles that address facilitation processes in evaluation work (Amba & Stake, 2001; House & Howe, 2000; King, 2007; King, Cousins, & Whitmore, 2007; King, Nielsen, & Colby, 2004; Rotondo, 2012), but none describe methods, techniques, or evaluation of facilitation in any detail.

The *American Journal of Evaluation* (AJE) publishes numerous articles related to organizational development and capacity building, along with articles on collaborative, participatory, empowerment, and democratic evaluation. While facilitation in each of these arenas is referenced, the discussion of approaches and techniques is neither broad nor deep. Little attention is given to evaluating facilitation itself. More notable is the December 2008 issue with articles discussing evaluation interactions (Cartland, Ruch-Ross, Mason, & Donohue 2008; Preskill & Boyle, 2008; Smits & Champagne, 2008). Other AJE issues with articles discussing facilitation include Cousins, Whitmore, and Shulha (2013); Friedman,

Rothman, and Withers (2006); and Preskill, Zukerman, and Matthews (2003), but again, description of approaches or techniques is limited.

Many resources are available on facilitation techniques and the skills involved (e.g., Bens, 2012; Hogan, 2002; Reddy, 1994, Schuman, 2005; Schwarz, 2002). They provide rich content and detail on various methods for working with groups, something not generally found in evaluation publications. However, the evaluation of facilitation work is not as widely used or written about as might be hoped. Two references noted above, by Reddy and by Schwarz, both cite evaluation of the facilitator, but provide little about the skills or competencies expected, or on what effect the implementation of these skills has on the group. These texts mention evaluation of a group's progress but provide no articulated framework for doing so. *Group Facilitation: A Research & Applications Journal*, beginning publication in 1999, is the primary academic periodical in the facilitation field, covering organizational learning and development, group and system dynamics, values, approaches, and the application of facilitation skills. It has included evaluation-related articles over the years, focusing initially on groups' decision-making processes and the impact of facilitators on group process (e.g., Shaw et al., 2010). In a recent issue, the *Journal* includes a more extensive article on facilitation interventions, outlining concepts on which to base evaluation, but without the detail to provide a comprehensive framework (Lichtenberg & London, 2008). Beyond the *Group Facilitation* journal, it is not easy to find published work about the evaluation of facilitation.

Definitions and Competencies

One of the dilemmas we faced in putting this issue together is the variety of definitions used for "facilitation." Merriam-Webster's 11th collegiate edition defines facilitation as "to make (something) easier; to help cause (something); to help (something) run more smoothly and effectively" (2005). The International Association of Facilitators (IAF), the group responsible for identifying standards for facilitator competencies, providing accreditation, and supporting facilitators and their development, does not explicitly define "facilitation" in its materials. This is, perhaps, testament to the different perspectives and interpretations of facilitation both as a philosophy and a set of tools or practices. The IAF's Statement of Values (adopted June, 2004), however, provides a characterization that likely will resonate with evaluators:

> As group facilitators, we believe in the inherent value of the individual and the collective wisdom of the group. We strive to help the group make the best use of the contributions of each of its members. We set aside our personal opinions and support the group's right to make its own choices. We believe that collaborative and cooperative interaction builds consensus and produces meaningful outcomes. We value professional collaboration to improve our profession.

NEW DIRECTIONS FOR EVALUATION • DOI: 10.1002/ev

In his forward to *The Facilitators Guide to Participatory Decision-Making* (Kaner, 2014), Michael Doyle noted the long history of facilitation and its beginnings as a formal process in the 1960s and 1970s along with the evolution of its definition over the years. Schwarz (2005) defined group facilitation as "a process in which a person whose selection is acceptable to all members of the group, who is substantively neutral, and who has no substantive decision-making authority diagnoses and intervenes to help a group improve how it identifies and solves problems and makes decisions, to increase the group's effectiveness" (p. 3). Hogan (2002) defined a facilitator as a "self-reflective, process-person who has a variety of human, process, technical skills and knowledge, together with a variety of experiences to assist groups of people to journey together to reach their goals." The International Institute of Facilitation and Change website (2013) includes a video that describes the dimensions of a facilitator's role as "architect, pilot, and guide." As one researcher in the field of facilitation put it (Thomas, 2008):

> To add to the confusion, the role that a facilitator plays has been likened to the conductor of an orchestra (Spencer, 1989, cited in Hogan, 2002); a catalyst, chameleon, and cabdriver (Priest, Gass, & Gillis, 2000); midwives (Hogan, 2002); a choreographer (Hunter, Bailey, & Taylor, 1995); and a change agent (Robson & Beary, 1995).

We can't agree more. We found that some authors contributing to this issue use a definition similar to Merriam-Webster's, but many had more nuanced versions when they considered their practices. We asked the authors to include a definition in their chapters to help us understand the theoretical perspectives from which they were working and to expand our thinking about what facilitation means.

As we began to explore our topic, we also saw that defining the skills of a facilitator, specifically those used in evaluation, was not so straightforward. "Facilitating constructive interpersonal interaction (teamwork, group facilitation, and processing)" is among the evaluator competencies identified in the AJE article, "Establishing Essential Competencies for Program Evaluators" (Stevahn, King, Ghere, & Minnema, 2005). Yet, detailed information on what actions or activities are a part of sound practice are not readily available, nor are facilitation techniques covered in any depth in most university curricula for evaluators. We may look to the IAF, which has identified knowledge, skills, and behaviors within its Core Facilitator Competencies and bases its certification process on them (www.iaf-world.org/Libraries/Certification_documents/Competencies.sflb.ashx).

The Structure of the Issue

Authors contributing to this issue represent both the evaluation and facilitation fields. Their practices span a range from sole practitioners and independent consulting firms to larger academic settings, with work ranging from single program–based projects to large-scale research and a broad variety of topics and clients. They describe grounding concepts that inform their work. They address culture, power, diversity, and inclusion and how they play out in group interaction. They talk about making choices on the methods to use depending on the client, context, and priorities of the work, as well as the practitioner's skill, confidence, and philosophy.

The issue is organized in three sections. The first includes two chapters focused on facilitation competencies and the skills considered elemental in an evaluation practice. These are followed by a more personal perspective on evaluation and facilitation and how it evolved for the author.

1. "Facilitating Evaluation to Lead Meaningful Change," by Tessie Tzavaras Catsambas of EnCompass, focuses on the skills and competencies for good facilitation in evaluation settings and a description of her experience leading in an evaluation of the African Science Academy Development Initiative of the U.S. National Academy of Sciences.
2. "Enhancing Facilitation Skills: Dancing with Dynamic Tensions," by Rita Sinorita Fierro of Fierro Consulting, examines facilitation skills in the context of the tensions that may occur in a group setting. She provides examples of how these tensions can play out and specific tips for dealing with them personally and in the group. Her chapter ends with a set of questions to help evaluators reflect on their facilitative practices.
3. "MĀRAMATANGA (Enlightenment): A Creative Approach to Connecting Facilitation and Evaluation," by Kataraina Pipi, an independent evaluator, talks about her entry into evaluation and the development of the "by Māori, for Māori" evaluation community and evaluation approaches. She provides an example of Planning Alternative Tomorrows with Hope (PATH) and shares an exercise she developed to support critical reflection, affirmation, and validation and describes how it could be used in personal planning, strategic planning, and evaluation.

   The second section of the issue focuses on the application of facilitation within evaluation, outlining specific steps in the process, strategies, and methods.
4. "Planning and Facilitating Working Sessions with Evaluation Stakeholders," by Rosalie T. Torres of the Torres Consulting Group, details 15 planning components of working sessions that can take place during evaluations, what may influence decisions about these components, and the facilitation issues to consider in each. The chapter includes a case example with the outcomes of a planning phase and subsequent working session, a description of issues that arose in the working session, and the facilitation approaches and techniques used to address these issues.

5. "Facilitating Interactive Evaluation Practice: Engaging Stakeholders Constructively," by Laurie Stevahn of Seattle University and Jean A. King of the University of Minnesota, describes interactive evaluation practice, its concepts of interaction in framing, implementing, and reporting evaluation, and the role of facilitation in the process. The chapter includes discussion of evaluator competencies related to facilitation, a set of interactive strategies and their uses, and a case example showing how these strategies were applied in two facilitated sessions to develop a program logic model.

6. "Data Placemats: A Facilitative Technique Designed to Enhance Stakeholder Understanding of Data," by Veena Pankaj and Ann K. Emery of the Innovation Network, shares a visual tool called data placemats, used as a facilitative technique in the analysis stage of evaluation as a means to enhance stakeholder understanding of evaluation data. The chapter shows when, why, and how to use data placemats and explores the connection between effective facilitation and implementation of this technique. It provides some sample data placemats, practical steps for evaluators in preparing for, facilitating, and following up on sessions using them, and examples of adapting the practice to different types of evaluations.

   The third section of the issue includes two chapters on the evaluation of facilitation—the first a proposed approach, the second a completed one.

7. "Evaluating Participatory Facilitated Conversations within the Art of Hosting Framework," by Alissa Schwartz of Solid Fire Consulting, uses the *Art of Hosting* and its methods for structuring meaningful conversations to outline an evaluation approach and methods that could be applied to facilitation. She provides a case example using a World Café session from the 2014 American Evaluation Conference in Denver.

8. "Invisible and Unbound? The Challenge and Practice of Evaluating Embedded Facilitation," by Jessica Dart, Managing Director, and Megan Roberts, Researcher, of Clear Horizon Consulting, describes a case study of the evaluation of Australian Landcare programs, a state-sponsored, community-driven natural resource management intervention. This 15-year effort uses government-funded facilitators to create opportunities for farmers to be involved in conservation on their land and with other land managers. The chapter provides a perspective on the challenges in evaluating facilitated interventions and practical ideas for addressing these challenges.

Our Conversations

In our conversations with authors throughout the process of developing this issue, we were aware of how much more there is to discuss, how much more we need to learn, and how much more we want to explore. Cataloging facilitation methods most useful at different steps in the evaluation process may be one avenue to pursue. Codifying facilitation competencies specific to evaluation is another. Perhaps most evident is the need to focus greater attention on the evaluation of facilitation and whether or how it benefits our work and our clients.

By becoming more skillful facilitators, evaluators can learn to sense, hear, and recognize both the dynamics in the room and the common threads among the perspectives and voices present. We can model productive, meaningful, and action-driven decision-making and evaluation processes. The most widely recognized resource for facilitation training is the IAF, serving as a repository for courses and workshops in its training directory. Yet many of the contributing authors shared that the ability to sense, listen deeply, capture group-generated information, reflect, and move groups toward action are more often learned through exposure to others' experiences. We hope this issue helps serve this purpose and expands the discussion, literature, and teaching around the connections between evaluation and facilitation.

We also believe that learning about different approaches to facilitation is of value, helping evaluators plan for facilitation activities. Some of the most familiar include:

- Appreciative Inquiry (http://appreciativeinquiry.case.edu/)
- Art of Hosting (http://www.artofhosting.org/)
- Cynefin Framework (Snowden, 2005)
- Deep Democracy (http://www.deepdemocracyinstitute.org/)
- Dynamic Facilitation (http://www.tobe.net/DF/dynamicfacilitation.html)
- Open Space (http://www.openspaceworld.org/)
- Theatre of the Oppressed (http://www.theatreoftheoppressed.org/en/index.php?nodeID=1)
- Theory U (https://www.presencing.com/theoryu)
- World Café (http://www.theworldcafe.com/)

To help make sense of the various methods and perspectives, the National Coalition for Dialogue & Deliberation (NCDD) created an "Engagement Streams Framework" that shows the differences among and pertinence of multiple facilitation methods (http://www.ncdd.org/files/rc/2014_Engagement_Streams_Guide_Print.pdf). We encourage evaluators to explore these resources and challenge our peers to experiment—to take some risks in trying new things.

We believe this issue will address the needs of experienced evaluators who feel the need for more reflection and skill building in facilitation and the needs of facilitators who are looking for evaluation frameworks that suit their work. We hope to expand the conversation about how these two practices affect each other by building the scholarship bridge between them.

We aim to propel evaluation and facilitation forward by deepening reflection about each of them.

References

Abma, T. A., & Stake, R. E. (2001). Stake's responsive evaluation: Core ideas and evolution. In J. C. Greene & T. A. Abma (Eds.), *Special Issue: Responsive evaluation. New Directions in Evaluation, 92,* 7–22.

Alkin, M. C., Daillak, R., & White, P. (1979). *Using evaluations: Does evaluation make a difference?* Beverly Hills, CA: Sage.

Appreciative Inquiry. (n.d.). Retrieved November 24, 2014, from http://appreciative inquiry.case.edu/

Art of Hosting. (n.d.). Retrieved November 24, 2014, from http://www.artofhosting.org/

Bens, I. (2012). *Facilitating with ease! Core skills for facilitators, team leaders and members, managers, consultants, and trainer* (3rd ed.). San Francisco, CA: Jossey-Bass.

Brandon, P. R., & Singh, J. M. (2009). The strengths of the methodological warrants for the findings on research on program evaluation use. *American Journal of Evaluation, 30,* 123–157.

Cartland, J., Ruch-Ross, H. S., Mason, M., & Donohue, W. (2008). Role sharing between evaluators and stakeholders in practice. *American Journal of Evaluation, 29,* 460–477.

Cousins, J. B., & Leithwood, K. A. (1986). Current empirical research in evaluation utilization. *Review of Educational Research, 56,* 331–364.

Cousins, J. B., Whitmore, E., & Shulha, L. (2013). Arguments for a common set of principles for collaborative inquiry in evaluation. *American Journal of Evaluation, 34,* 7–22.

Deep Democracy International. (n.d.). Retrieved November 24, 2014, from http://www .deepdemocracyinstitute.org/deep-democracy-institute.html

Deutsch, M. (1949a). A theory of cooperation and competition. *Human Relations, 2,* 129–151.

Deutsch, M. (1949b). An experimental study of the effects of cooperation and competition upon group processes. *Human Relations, 2,* 199–231.

Deutsch, M. (1973). *The resolution of conflict: Constructive and destructive processes.* New Haven, CT: Yale University Press.

Deutsch, M. (2006). Cooperation and competition. In M. Deutsch, P. T. Coleman, & E. C. Marcus (Eds.), *The handbook of conflict resolution: Theory and practice* (2nd ed., pp. 23–42). San Francisco, CA: Jossey-Bass.

Dynamic Facilitation. (n.d.). Retrieved November 24, 2014, from http://www.tobe.net /DF/dynamicfacilitation.html

Easterby-Smith, M., Crossan, M., & Nicolini, D. (2000). Organizational learning: Debates past, present and future. *Journal of Management Studies, 37,* 784–796.

Fiol, C. M., & Lyes, M. A. (1985). Organizational learning, *The Academy of Management Review, 10,* 803–813.

Friedman, V. J., Rothman, J., & Withers, B. (2006). The power of why: Engaging the goal paradox in program evaluation. *American Journal of Evaluation, 27,* 201–218.

Hogan, C. F. (2002). *Understanding facilitation: Theory and principles: A toolkit of techniques.* London, UK: Kogan Page.

House, E. R., & Howe, K. R. (2000). Deliberative democratic evaluation. In K. E. Ryan & L. DeStefano (Eds.), *Special Issue: Evaluation as a democratic process: Promoting inclusion, dialogue, and deliberation. New Directions in Evaluation, 85,* 3–12.

Huber, G. P. (1991). Organizational learning: The contributing processes and literatures. *Organizational Science, 2,* 88–115.

Hunter, D., Bailey, A., & Taylor, B. (1999). *The essence of facilitation: Being in action in groups.* Auckland, New Zealand: Tandem Press.

International Institute of Facilitation and Change. (2013) *What Do Facilitators Do*. Retrieved November 24, 2014, from http://english.iifac.org/

International Association of Facilitators. (2004, June). *Statement of Values and Code of Ethics*. Retrieved September 19, 2014, from http://www.iaf-world.org/AboutIAF/CodeofEthics.aspx

Johnson, D. W., & Johnson, F. P. (2009). *Joining together: Group theory and group skills* (10th ed.). Boston, MA: Pearson Education Allyn & Bacon.

Johnson, D. W., & Johnson, R. T. (1989). *Cooperation and competition: Theory and research*. Edina, MN: Interaction Book Company.

Johnson, D. W., & Johnson, R. T. (2005). New developments in social interdependence theory. *Genetic, Social, and General Psychology Monographs, 131*, 285–358.

Johnson, D. W., Johnson, R. T., & Stevahn, L. (2011). Social interdependence and program evaluation. In M. M. Mark, S. I. Donaldson, & B. Campbell (Eds.), *Social psychology and evaluation* (pp. 288–317). New York, NY: Guilford Press.

Johnson, K., Greenseid, L. O., Toal, S. A., King, J. A., Lawrenz, F., & Volkov, B. (2009). Research on evaluation use: A review of the empirical literature from 1986 to 2005. *American Journal of Evaluation, 30*, 377–410.

Kaner, S. (2014). *The facilitator's guide to participatory decision-making* (3rd ed.). San Francisco, CA: Jossey-Bass.

King, J. A. (2007). Developing evaluation capacity through process use. In J. B. Cousins (Ed.), *Special Issue: Process use in theory, research, and practice. New Directions in Evaluation, 116*, 45–69.

King, J. A., Cousins, J. B., & Whitmore, E. (2007). Making sense of participatory evaluation: Framing participatory evaluation. In S. Mathison (Ed.), *Special Issue: Enduring issues in evaluation: The 20th anniversary of the collaboration between NDE and AEA. New Directions in Evaluation, 114*, 83–105.

King, J. A., Nielsen, J. E., & Colby, J. (2004). Lessons for culturally competent evaluation from the study of a multicultural initiative. In M. Thompson-Robinson, R Hopson, & S. SenGupta (Eds.), *Special Issue: In search of cultural competence in evaluation: Toward principles and practices. New Directions in Evaluation, 102*, 67–80.

King, J. A., & Pechman, E. M. (1984). Pinning a wave to the shore: Conceptualizing school evaluation use. *Educational Evaluation and Policy Analysis, 6*, 241–251.

Kirkhart, K. E. (2000). Reconceptualizing evaluation use: An integrated theory of influence. In V. Caracelli & H. Preskill (Eds.), *The expanding scope of evaluation use. New Directions for Evaluation, 88*, 5–23.

Lewin, K. (1947). Frontiers in group dynamics: II. Channels of group life; social planning and action research. *Human Relations, 1*, 143–153.

Lewin, K. (1953). Studies in group decision. In D. Cartwright & A. Zander (Eds.), *Group dynamics, research and theory* (pp. 287–301). Evanston, IL: Row, Peterson and Company.

Lichtenberg, J., & London, M. (2008). Evaluating group interventions: A framework for diagnosing, implementing, and evaluating group interventions. *Group Facilitation: A Research & Application Journal, 9*, 37–48.

Merriam-Webster online dictionary. 11th collegiate edition. (n.d.). Facilitation. Retrieved September 19, 2014, from http://www.m-w.com/dictionary/facilitation

National Coalition for Dialogue & Deliberation. (n.d.). Retrieved November 24, 2014, from http://www.ncdd.org

Open Space. (n.d.). Retrieved November 24, 2014, from http://www.openspaceworld.org/

Ottoson, J., & Martinez, D. (2010). *An ecological understanding of evaluation use. A case study for the* Active for Life *evaluation* Princeton, NJ: Robert Wood Johnson Foundation. Retrieved from http://www.rwjf.org/files/research/71148.ottoson.final.pdf

Patton, M. Q. (2008). *Utilization-focused evaluation* (4th ed.). Thousand Oaks, CA: Sage.

Patton, M. Q. (2012). *Essentials of utilization-focused evaluation*. Thousand Oaks, CA: Sage.

Preskill, H., & Boyle, S. (2008). A multidisciplinary model of evaluation capacity building. *American Journal of Evaluation, 29,* 443–459.

Preskill, H., & Caracelli, V. (1997). Current and developing conceptions of use: Evaluation use TIG survey results. Evaluation Practice, 18, 209–225.

Preskill, H., Zukerman, B., & Matthews, B. (2003). An exploratory study of process use: Findings and implications for future research. *American Journal of Evaluation, 24,* 423–442.

Reddy, W. B. (1994). *Intervention skills, process consultation for small groups and teams.* San Francisco, CA: Jossey-Bass.

Rotondo, E. (2012). Lessons learned from evaluation capacity building. In S. Kushner & E. Rotondo (Eds.), *Special Issue: Evaluation voices from Latin America. New Directions in Evaluation, 134,* 93–101.

Schuman. S. (2005). *The IAF handbook of group facilitation: Best practices from the leading organization in facilitation.* San Francisco, CA: Jossey-Bass.

Schwarz, R. (2002). *The skilled facilitator: A comprehensive resource for consultants, facilitators, managers, trainers, and coaches* (2nd ed.). San Francisco, CA: Jossey-Bass.

Schwarz, R. (2005). The skilled facilitator approach. In R. Schwarz & A. Davidson (Eds.), *The skilled facilitator fieldbook: Tips, tools, and tested methods for consultants, facilitators, managers, trainers, and coaches* (pp. 3–13). San Francisco, CA: Jossey-Bass.

Scott, B. B. (2011). *Organizational learning: A literature review* (Discussion Paper #2011–02). Available from Queen's University IRC, IRC Research Program, irc.queensu.ca.

Shaw, E., Looney, A., Chase, S., Navalekar, R., Stello, B., Lontok, O., & Crabtree, B. (2010). "In the Moment": An analysis of facilitator impact during a quality improvement process. *Group Facilitation: A Research & Application Journal, 10,* 4–16.

Shula, L. M., & Cousins, J. B. (1997). Evaluation use: Theory, research, and practice since 1986. *Evaluation Practice, 18,* 195–208.

Smits, P., & Champagne, F. (2008). An assessment of the theoretical underpinnings of practical participatory evaluation. *American Journal of Evaluation, 29,* 427–442.

Snowden, D. (2005). Multi-ontology sense making—A new simplicity in decision making. *Informatics in Primary Health Care, 13:* 45–53.

Stevahn, L., King, J. A., Ghere, G., & Minnema, J. (2005). Establishing essential competencies for program evaluators. *American Journal of Evaluation, 26,* 43–59.

Theatre of the Oppressed. (n.d.). Retrieved November 24, 2014, from http://www.theatreoftheoppressed.org/en/index.php?nodeID=1

Theory U. (n.d.). Retrieved November 24, 2014, from https://www.presencing.com/theoryu

Thomas, G. (2008). A study of the theories and practices of facilitator educators: Conclusions from a naturalistic inquiry. *Group Facilitation: A Research & Application Journal, 8,* 4–13.

Weick, K. E., & Westley, F. (1996). Organizational learning: Affirming an oxymoron. In S. R. Clegg, C. Hardy, & W. R. Nord (Eds.), *Handbook of organization studies,* (pp. 440–458). London, UK: Sage.

Weiss, C. H. (1972). *Evaluating action programs: Readings in social action and education.* Boston, MA: Allyn & Bacon.

Weiss, C. H. (1998). Have we learned anything new about the use of evaluation? *American Journal of Evaluation, 19,* 21–33.

World Café. (n.d.). Retrieved November 24, 2014, from http://www.theworldcafe.com/

Rita Sinorita Fierro
Alissa Schwartz
Dawn Hanson Smart

RITA S. FIERRO, PhD, is the founder of Fierro Consulting, LLC, a firm working for national and international organizations, nonprofits, foundations, and innovative businesses in North America, Europe, New Zealand, and Africa that uses facilitation, evaluation, and research to help inspire individuals, groups, and communities to thrive in excellence while they pursue their goals together.

ALISSA SCHWARTZ, MSW, PhD, is an independent organizational consultant with a practice in participatory facilitation, program evaluation, leadership development, and strategy planning. You can learn more about her work from her website: www.solidfireconsulting.com.

DAWN HANSON SMART is an independent consultant focused on collaboration and participatory work in evaluation, strategic planning, organizational development and capacity-building with nonprofits, foundations, and local and state government.

NEW DIRECTIONS FOR EVALUATION • DOI: 10.1002/ev

Catsambas, T. T. (2016). Facilitating evaluation to lead meaningful change . In R. S. Fierro, A. Schwartz, & D. H. Smart (Eds.), *Evaluation and Facilitation. New Directions for Evaluation, 149*, 19–29.

1

Facilitating Evaluation to Lead Meaningful Change

Tessie Tzavaras Catsambas

Abstract

Evaluation education and training has traditionally emphasized methodological skills and ignored soft skills. A review of routine evaluation tasks, however, reveals that evaluation typically requires the evaluator to work with groups of people for organizing and managing an evaluation, as well as in collecting and analyzing data; that is, evaluators must frequently facilitate group interactions to conclude an evaluation successfully. A juxtaposition of evaluator and facilitator competencies shows significant overlap between them. Furthermore, evaluations of increasing complexity call for higher levels of facilitation. Transformational evaluations call for significant self-development and strengthening of leadership competencies. Through development and use of facilitation tools and techniques, facilitation can be used to enhance the effectiveness and use of an evaluation. © 2016 Wiley Periodicals, Inc., and the American Evaluation Association.

What Does It Mean to "Facilitate" Evaluation?

Evaluation is an intervention and a process, one that requires the facilitation of interactions at multiple steps along the way. The evaluator engages in facilitation throughout the course of an evaluation, beginning with negotiating the terms of reference, contract agreement, appropriate permissions, participation of those who fund the evaluation, and those who are evaluated or are otherwise affected by the evaluation. So the question is not whether evaluators facilitate process and relationships, it is how well they do so. Evaluators need to understand how facilitation influences evaluation outcomes, assess their own level of facilitation competence, and determine appropriate paths for enhancing their facilitation skills for evaluation.

In considering the role of facilitation in evaluation, Michael Doyle provides a striking definition of a facilitator as "content neutral"—someone who does not promote a particular point of view but rather advocates for "fair, open, and inclusive procedures to accomplish the group's work" (Kaner et al., 2007, p. xiii). This essential aspect of the facilitator's role is also important in evaluation. In their role, evaluators engage in the following activities:

• bring a structure for engaging clients and stakeholders, grounded in their evaluation methodology (e.g., planning meetings or conducting interviews, focus groups, and surveys);
• contribute to the potential effectiveness of teams by offering them accurate and reliable data that are easy to understand and use in making decisions and improving programs and organizational performance; and
• remain independent, aiming to include different perspectives in the evaluation without taking sides.

There is wide consensus in the evaluation community about the importance of conducting useful evaluations (see, for example, Patton, 2008, and Fetterman, Kaftarian, & Wandersman, 1995) in which the potential for use is built in from the beginning and discussed in the planning stages. Patton and Fetterman each write of the need to incorporate participatory methods to ensure that evaluation responds to the burning questions of program implementers; in this way, evaluation becomes relevant for evaluation clients—those who fund the evaluation, and those who are evaluated.

In collecting data, evaluators know the importance of facilitation skills in creating a safe space to elicit honest and complete feedback. Focus group guidance calls for a facilitator or researcher who will enable participants to feel "respected, comfortable, and free to give their opinions without being judged" (Krueger & Casey, 2009, p. 4). Furthermore, some evaluations require the evaluator to help clients understand, accept, and make use of the results, a stipulation that places further demands for facilitation on evaluators. Good facilitation of the evaluation process increases client engagement and buy-in, fosters a safe place for honesty, and creates a neutral space for airing different views with an impartial and independent evaluator. When an evaluation is complex or controversial, good facilitation enables the evaluator to receive more honest inputs and to challenge assumptions without getting participants so angry that they disengage from the evaluation.

What Does "Facilitation" Mean in Evaluation?

Put simply, every part of every evaluation that involves contact with people needs to be facilitated. It follows, therefore, that the more skilled evaluators are in facilitation, the more effective they will be in working through the issues and challenges that arise during typical evaluations. Patton (2011) makes this need clear, suggesting (somewhat wryly) that the evaluation is much enhanced when the evaluator is

> A skilled communicator, an excellent facilitator, culturally sensitive, methodologically competent and eclectic, manifesting a strong tolerance for ambiguity, flexible and responsive, and fundamentally a good person—that is, an all-round saintly type with exemplary character. (p. 68)

Despite acknowledgement of the importance of facilitation by some of evaluation's most prominent practitioners, evaluation instruction has traditionally emphasized methods, leaving out facilitation competencies even as many methods explicitly require those competencies. Limited instruction has left many evaluators to their own devices to figure out what facilitation skills they need, and how to develop them.

With so many facilitation techniques available, their use depends on the objective of the assignment and on the style, skill, and sophistication of the facilitator. As evaluators, how do we select the skills we need to support our work? Let us review facilitation at three levels of sophistication and examine the intersection with evaluation at each level.

Level 1: "Basic" Facilitation

In facilitation's simplest form, we might imagine a pleasant person in front of a room helping participants get along and get their work done. In fact, even basic facilitation—just like evaluation—is a complex field with different schools of thought, conceptual models, frameworks, and tools. The International Association of Facilitators (IAF) has a list of competencies it requires of trained facilitators; these competencies are important for evaluators as well.

Table 1.1 demonstrates a clear relationship between facilitation and evaluation competencies and a definite link between facilitator competencies and several of the American Evaluation Association's (AEA's) guiding principles. Just like facilitators, evaluators have to build and maintain constructive relationships with stakeholders, manage engagement with people (e.g., for evaluation steering committee meetings, focus groups, and group

Table 1.1. Correspondence Between Facilitator and Evaluator Competencies

IAF[a] facilitation competencies	Relevant IDEAS[b] evaluation competencies	Relevant AEA[c] guiding principles
Create collaborative client relationships	Builds and maintains constructive relationships with partners, evaluation commissioners, and other stakeholders	Evaluators respect the security, dignity, and self-worth of respondents, program participants, clients, and other evaluation stakeholders
Plan appropriate group processes	Undertakes appropriate upfront exploration and planning for an evaluation, including stakeholder engagement	Ensure that the evaluation team collectively possesses the education, abilities, skills, and experience appropriate to the evaluation
Create and sustain a participatory environment[b]	Displays appropriate cross-cultural competencies and cultural sensitivity	Ensure that the evaluation team collectively demonstrates cultural competence and uses appropriate evaluation strategies and skills to work with culturally different groups
Guide group to appropriate useful outcomes	Develops or assists in developing the strongest feasible design to answer the evaluation questions and respond to the evaluation's purpose. Provides guidance to others within and external to the organization on development evaluation planning and design, methods, and approaches	Provide competent services to stakeholders. In addition, this facilitator competency particularly resonates with facilitators concerned with evaluation
Build and maintain professional knowledge	Knows literature, concepts, and methods, participates in professional networks, and works toward self-improvement	Seek to maintain and improve their competencies in order to provide the highest level of performance in their evaluations
Model positive professional attitude	Knows the IDEAS Code of Ethics and behaves in accord with it[e]	Integrity and honesty[d]

[a]International Association of Facilitators.
[b]International Development Evaluation Association.
[c]American Evaluation Association.
[d]This IAF core competency includes the need to "cultivate cultural awareness and sensitivity".
[e]The Code of Ethics is extensive, covering honesty, conflict of interest, empowering stakeholders, promoting equity, and so forth.

interviews), maintain a participatory environment within and across cultures, and achieve results.

Beyond the core competencies, facilitators—just as evaluators—continue to add new knowledge and skills through different methods, such as:

- *Open Space*, a method for engaging groups to define the agenda they wish to address and self-manage subsequent conversations (Owen, 2008);
- *Future Search*, a "task-focused" method that "helps people transform their capability for action very quickly" (Weisbord & Janoff, 2010, p. 1);
- The *Art of Convening*, which seeks to bring "authentic engagement and authentic leadership in … meetings, gatherings, and conversations" (Neal & Neal, 2011, p. xiii);
- *Appreciative Inquiry*, a process that directs respondents to study success (Preskill & Catsambas, 2006); and
- *World Café*, a group-engagement method used to foster increased understanding, learning, or common ground (Brown, 2005).

Whatever methods facilitators adopt, the core competencies are similar and include the same ingredients—relationships, communication, participation, respect, asking good questions, ethics, engagement, and quality—every one of which also matters for evaluation.

Level 2: "Advanced" Facilitation

As one may expect, more demanding situations—dealing with an organization's senior leaders, groups experiencing hostility, post-conflict trauma, and other challenges, for example—require higher levels of competence. To perform well in such cases, facilitators need not only advanced skills, but also a high level of self-development. Advanced facilitators have "done their own work" to reach high levels of authenticity, self-awareness, and self-management.

More challenging evaluations require similarly advanced facilitation competencies, particularly competencies in leadership development and coaching. Why should we, as evaluators and facilitators of evaluation, care about leadership development? In complex and challenging situations, there is a convergence of roles—evaluation, facilitation, leadership development, executive coaching, and organizational development—around the common goal of enabling our clients and evaluands to understand their situation and shape a constructive way forward based on reliable evidence.

When evaluators work on complex issues characterized by political sensitivity, conflict, or other challenges, or with groups that do not get along, they need to have the fortitude and ability to navigate through to a successful evaluation. This is all the more important when we seek to engage in "transformative" evaluation.

Level 3: Facilitation for "Transformative" Evaluation

One type of complex evaluation goes beyond usefulness, aiming to catalyze change in clients, stakeholders, and society as a whole. Several leading evaluation thinkers call for this type of complexity in equity-focused, developmental, and "transformative" evaluation. Mertens (2009) suggests that the evaluator's role is a transformative one, which seeks to promote social justice by intervening in what Chambers (2012) has called the "perpetual tension between a dominant paradigm of things and a subordinate paradigm of people" (p. xv). In such cases, evaluators are challenged to think carefully about the role they see themselves playing.

What kind of facilitation competencies do we need to engage in transformative evaluation—to become, as Schaetti, Ramsey, and Watanabe (2008) suggest, "skilled change agents"? Patton (2008) suggests we engage in "reflective practice," and Mertens (2009) agrees, suggesting that we need more than skills and techniques: we need self-knowledge and cultural knowledge. We want to challenge program managers and policy makers to think evaluatively, strategically, systemically, and clearly. To think differently takes abilities beyond one discipline, so that one can see the links between inputs and broader impact, listen for understanding, and overcome resistance to ideas that do not fit into existing paradigms. Thinking differently also means having the courage to raise difficult issues, acknowledge limitations in oneself and make changes, and the ability to communicate a compelling vision. How else can we find the voice to raise issues our clients may wish to ignore, in ways that increase their capacity to listen and change, while empowering those who have been silent to speak up?

Challenging Evaluators to Become Skilled Facilitators

This discussion of the intersection of facilitation and evaluation is incomplete without a look at practice. To help me think through this question, I spoke with Michael Quinn Patton and Donna Mertens. Patton, who has worked recently on evaluation competencies for leaders, is known for incorporating systems thinking and creative facilitation in his work. Mertens is a leading thinker in transformative evaluation who boldly pushes for self-development in her courses. Working in different spheres and with different styles, Patton and Mertens each challenge those they train in evaluation to go to places of discomfort, aiming to bring about some level of transformative personal growth that, ultimately, helps participants become skilled facilitators. High-level facilitation skills enable the evaluator both to get out of the way and to push people and organizations to make their own decisions and find a way forward.

NEW DIRECTIONS FOR EVALUATION • DOI: 10.1002/ev

"It's All Data": Facilitating Reflection in Evaluation Training

For Patton, the link between evaluation and facilitation is so obvious that he calls himself a "facilitator of evaluation," rather than an evaluator. He always teaches aspects of facilitation when he teaches evaluation, organizing people in "learning circles" where he encourages them to ask systems questions to find out what is known and unknown. Participants practice interviewing, and he tells them to "listen long enough so they might begin to understand" (M. Patton, personal communication, April 24, 2014).

Patton described a tough facilitation challenge he had experienced while conducting a workshop on qualitative methods for 12 senior ministry staff (of an unnamed country) who had been sent to his workshop without being consulted. When Patton asked them to participate in an exercise at the start of the workshop, they stayed seated, arms crossed, with clearly hostile body language. He was shocked—this had never happened to him before—but he persevered. Showing nothing to the group, he told himself, "it's all data." With that mind-set, he asked the group to tell him what was going on. The participants voiced their frustration with the "useless" workshops their minister regularly imposed on them. On the spot, Patton offered to work with them to do a collaborative, qualitative assessment of the practice of workshops, and develop a participatory report with their analysis and suggestions for the minister.

Patton's story shows us that, in the moment, when the facilitator/evaluator is under significant pressure and attracting a lot of negative emotions, it is the advanced competencies of self-knowledge, courage, and reflective practice that get him or her through to a constructive place. Strong facilitator skills help the evaluator not to take sides or defend when attacked, but to turn that negative energy around, using it as data, in a process of discovery.

Facilitation: A "Neglected Area" in Evaluation

In reflecting on the intersection of evaluation and facilitation, especially from the perspective of transformative research, Donna Mertens called facilitation "a neglected area" of evaluation practice. She believes that engagement with people is something that must occur before an evaluation's purpose can be established. First, we need to ask ourselves, "How do I approach people in ways that are appropriate given culture, status, and power?" (D. Mertens, personal communication, April 25, 2014).

For Mertens, having facilitation competencies is a minimum requirement for evaluators. She calls for self-awareness—knowing the answer to the questions, "Who am I?" and "Who am I in relation to this community?" She wants you, the evaluator, to think about what you will do when something makes you uncomfortable. Mertens pushes her students' transformation in every way possible: through action research, homework that asks for interaction with others, and role-plays in the classroom. For example, she teaches a group on evaluation related to gender discrimination and disability in Brazil, Albania, and other countries. Mertens requires her students to go into communities to explore cultural constructions of disability, review the status of relevant legislation, and investigate any actions the country has taken. In essence, these students are engaged in transformative action research. In meeting community organizations, they are working to suspend their assumptions so they can really see what is going on, and then to structure evaluation in ways that enables those being evaluated to engage with evaluation more openly and courageously. Their evaluation work is leading up to an action plan, and the alliances they are developing along the way help them find out what works, and what should be done.

Mertens, like other experts (see, for example, Heifetz, Grashow, & Linsky, 2009), recognizes that no single technique will give a facilitator (or an evaluator) the skills to suspend judgment and listen deeply, the fortitude to listen to attacks calmly, or the courage to challenge the status quo.

Marvin Weisbord, who developed the Future Search methodology, entitled his most recent facilitation book, *Don't Just Do Something, Stand There: Ten Principles for Leading Meetings That Matter* (Weisbord & Janoff, 2007). The title is one of Weisbord's favorite challenges to facilitators—something that is very hard to do without self-discipline and self-confidence. That is exactly what Patton and Mertens want to instill in evaluators.

Facilitation to Reframe the Theory of Change: The ASADI Evaluation

In exploring the link between evaluation and facilitation, I find it useful to reflect on my experience as project manager of an independent evaluation of the African Science Academy Development Initiative (ASADI). In this example, facilitated evaluation processes helped project implementers transform their perception of theory of change, partner roles, and priorities, which led to effective changes in their strategy and relationships, and, in turn, resulted in improved program outcomes that surpassed expectations.

Launched in 2004 to foster a more evidence-based approach to health and development on the African continent, ASADI was funded by the Bill and Melinda Gates Foundation and implemented by the National Academy of Sciences (NAS), which was seen as an excellent model for ASADI. NAS initially selected three academies in Nigeria, South Africa, and Uganda for higher funding and intensive technical assistance. The plan was to transfer lessons from these three main partners once they became stronger institutions that could teach their counterparts in other African countries.

Early on, NAS issued a call for proposals for a "highly participatory" independent evaluation to support learning through evaluation as NAS refined its theory of change. NAS wanted to monitor the experience of African academies and develop their evaluation capacity. My company, EnCompass LLC, and a South African firm, OtherWISE, were selected to carry out the evaluation. As project manager, I worked closely with the NAS team and with ASADI Director Dr. Patrick Kelley. The perceptions presented here represent my reflections on the role of facilitation in this evaluation project.

At the end of the first year, the evaluation team had gathered important findings that challenged assumptions in NAS's theory of change. When NAS asked for a first-year evaluation report, we asked for a facilitated meeting to review the findings jointly and come up with interpretations and recommendations together. Our assessment was that our findings would be seen as critical of the hard work of the NAS and that our client would not know how to use it constructively; a facilitated meeting, however, would offer the NAS the opportunity to consider our findings gradually and through a new lens of self-analysis, thus leading to constructive use of findings. The agenda for the meeting incorporated several facilitation methods (listed in parentheses):

- Appreciative interviews to reflect on successful aspects of ASADI and explore existing interventions (Appreciative Inquiry, Values Analysis, and Visioning)
- Identification and in-depth discussion of issues (Reflective Practice)
- Revisiting the role of evaluation for ASADI (modified Johari Window)
- Reflection on the day (Reflective Practice)

Several important things happened during that heavily facilitated session. As we reviewed participants' experiences and data from the field from the first year, we began together to challenge and abandon a few key assumptions in ASADI's original theory of change. Dr. Kelley and NAS's advisors had already experienced the shock of administrative complexities of working in Africa (e.g., how many steps are involved in making even one simple decision, resistance to early planning for conferences, etc.). In some cases, they had gotten stuck trying to figure out administrative matters rather than doing programmatic work. In several academies, processes took significantly longer than expected and, rather than focusing on scientific and professional discourse, NAS staff had sometimes found themselves in the unpleasant and unfulfilling role of policing administrative practices.

The breakthrough in this one-day session came from using the data the evaluation team had collected and facilitating NAS staff to step out of their own shoes and imagine how their African colleagues were experiencing them. NAS staff surprised the evaluation team with their insights from the reflective practice. Two of their conclusions in particular demonstrated how significantly participants reconsidered their assumptions about the African academies as a result of the facilitated day. First, as implementation of ASADI unfolded, the African academies, their governments, and NAS staff all experienced a deepened appreciation of the value of creating a trusting partnership. Second, as differences in culture and work habits made it necessary to stop and address unanticipated issues, staff from NAS and the African academies began to understand the need for shared values (such as transparency, collaboration, valuing of women, and seniority) as a precursor to the specific technical assistance that had formed a large part of the initial theory of change.

After that first-year meeting, the NAS team often slipped into a "reflection space" during meetings to monitor progress or prepare for evaluation team site visits. Dr. Kelley once joked that they saw me as their "evaluator/psychologist." When the time came for the final report, Dr. Kelley asked instead for individual reports for the three academies, because he valued the independent voice of the evaluation and the insight it gave him into the perspective of each African academy.

Reflecting later on the facilitation aspect of the ASADI evaluation, Dr. Kelley told me,

> You were effective at understanding the theory of change of what we were trying to do. You helped me organize my thoughts about what was needed in ASADI. When we started, it seem[ed] that everything needed to be done. We did not have a route to change. We thought we would do all these things simultaneously. ... You were helpful in giving us a high-level approach to see how we were organizing our work. [After the facilitated meeting,] we listened to and truly understood the African academies. (P. Kelley, personal communication, April 24, 2014)

After that first year, Dr. Kelley and his team refocused their efforts on board development, bringing African academy scientists to their headquarters for consultations, building relationships, and developing shared visions. By the end of the grant, many ASADI academies—their number grew as the project evolved—went on to be very successful, and most have become sustainable.

Conclusion

At a minimum, evaluators need basic facilitation skills to organize, negotiate, and carry out an evaluation. Experienced facilitators and organizational development experts consistently employ deliberate, structured, and experiential processes that enable groups and individuals to strengthen awareness of the self and others, develop a deeper understanding of issues (in an organization or a program), discover common ground among stakeholders, and work together constructively toward a desired future that is expressed in measurable outcomes and feasible recommendations. Evaluators may often find themselves in situations in which they have to "facilitate" their way through political sensitivities, misunderstandings, competing interests, confusion, apathy, or refusal to cooperate. To reach their highest level of effectiveness, evaluators should cultivate advanced skills in facilitation, and if possible, leadership development and executive coaching. Evaluators can

NEW DIRECTIONS FOR EVALUATION • DOI: 10.1002/ev

benefit from these competencies not only to be effective in their work, but also to advance their personal and professional development.

References

Brown, J. (2005). *The World Café: Shaping our futures through conversations that matter.* San Francisco, CA: Berrett-Koehler.

Chambers, R. (2012). *Provocations for development.* Warwickshire, UK: Practical Action.

Fetterman, D. F., Kaftarian, S. J., & Wandersman, A. (Eds.). (1995). *Empowerment evaluation: Knowledge and tools for self-assessment and accountability.* Thousand Oaks, CA: Sage.

Heifetz, R. A., Grashow, A., & Linsky, M. (2009). *The practice of adaptive leadership: Tools and tactics for changing your organization and the world.* Boston, MA: Harvard Business Press.

Kaner, S., Lind, L., Toldi, C., Fisk, S., & Berger, D. (2007). *Facilitator's guide to participatory decision-making.* San Francisco, CA: Jossey-Bass/Wiley.

Krueger, R., & Casey, M. (2009). *Focus groups: A practical guide for applied research.* Thousand Oaks, CA: Sage.

Mertens, D. (2009). *Transformative research and evaluation.* New York, NY: Guilford Press.

Neal, C., & Neal, P. (2011). *The art of convening: Authentic engagement in meetings, gatherings, and conversations.* San Francisco, CA: Berrett-Koehler.

Owen, H. (2008). *Open Space Technology: A user's guide.* San Francisco, CA: Berrett-Koehler.

Patton, M. (2008). *Utilization-focused evaluation* (4th ed.). Thousand Oaks, CA: Sage.

Patton, M. (2011). *Developmental evaluation: Applying complexity to enhance innovation and use.* New York, NY: Guildford Press.

Preskill, H., & Catsambas, T. (2006). *Reframing evaluation through appreciative inquiry.* Thousand Oaks, CA: Sage.

Schaetti, B. F., Ramsey, S. J., & Watanabe, G. C. (2008). *Personal leadership: Making a world of difference: A methodology of two principles and six practices.* Seattle, WA: Flying Kite.

Weisbord, M., & Janoff, S. (2007). *Don't just do something, stand there! Ten principles for leading meetings that matter.* San Francisco, CA: Berrett-Koehler.

Weisbord, M., & Janoff, S. (2010). *Future Search: Getting the whole system in the room for vision, commitment, and action.* San Francisco, CA: Berrett-Koehler.

TESSIE TZAVARAS CATSAMBAS, president of EnCompass LLC, is an evaluation and organizational development expert with more than 25 years' experience in evaluation, quality improvement, and innovation.

NEW DIRECTIONS FOR EVALUATION • DOI: 10.1002/ev

Fierro, R. S. (2016). Enhancing facilitation skills: Dancing with dynamic tensions. In R. S. Fierro, A. Schwartz, & D. H. Smart (Eds.), *Evaluation and Facilitation. New Directions for Evaluation, 149*, 31–42.

2

Enhancing Facilitation Skills: Dancing with Dynamic Tensions

Rita Sinorita Fierro

Abstract

For evaluators there is a high price for bad facilitation: Without our knowing, we may favor our own priorities, forget participants' needs, submerge stakeholder voices, hide underlying causes, and undermine the impact of our work. The author shows how to improve one's facilitation skills by leveraging seven dynamic tensions: Hosting self and others, hosting present and absent stakeholders, observing group and individual dynamics, simplifying and unveiling complexity, listening and sensing emergence, using intuition and rational problem solving, and facing chaos and control. © 2016 Wiley Periodicals, Inc., and the American Evaluation Association.

Facilitation can be a tricky topic. Is it a discipline? A practice? Is it as natural a function to human beings as walking or talking? Or is it an acquired skill? An art? Facilitation is all of the above: both a natural and an acquired skill, art, and discipline. One can facilitate an informal lively discussion at a dinner table without formal training with common sense, tact, and listening skills. But the more diverse participants are, the higher the expectations and the stakes; and the wider the gap between people's perspectives, the more complex facilitating can be.

The conversations we find ourselves facilitating as evaluators are often of this complex nature. Funding, salaries, and professional reputations are at stake. Tensions are heightened. Communities struggle for power and control. Politicians are up for reelection. We are often pressed to "prove" positive impact before results are certain.

In high-pressure contexts, evaluators often think forward to the next activity. *Where are the Post-its? Is the board ready? Do I have enough time for this activity?* In our evaluation training programs in the United States, we most often stress linear logic models (inputs to long-term outcomes) and linear evaluation designs (planning to dissemination). Linear thinking encourages us to look ahead. We have an idea of the ideal process, outcomes to reporting, and even when we do things collaboratively, our focus is on pushing the process forward.

Pushing ahead makes us feel accomplished at the end of the meeting, but we can gain a false sense of security and lose touch with what is actually happening in the group. When as evaluators we disconnect from the participants' needs to favor our own priorities, stakeholder voices get submerged, underlying factors stay hidden, and systemic challenges to the achievement of our objectives continue to undermine the impact of the work without us knowing it. Some stakeholders who don't value our evaluation framework can sabotage the evaluation at a later date. Tensions among stakeholders can surface and, if inappropriately addressed, can bring forth retaliation from people with more formal power.

In this chapter, I identify ways evaluators who facilitate can improve their facilitation skills by accepting and leveraging opposite priorities that may occur in a group setting. Becoming more aware of group dynamics can help evaluators be present to what is happening in the moment and bring added benefits to the group and the evaluation. Practicing these skills can help evaluators allow groups more discretion over *where* they want to go together and *how* to get there. These skills are especially useful to evaluators who use collaborative, participatory, and capacity-building methodologies, because when the number of stakeholders involved in evaluation increases, so does the complexity. These skills can also benefit evaluators who use other approaches, since facilitation can take place in meeting with only one stakeholder such as a client or program manager. First, I will review definitions of the terms *creative tension*, *polarity*, and *dynamic tension*, then define how "facilitation" is being used in this chapter.

The Facilitation Challenge: Creative Tension and Emotional Tension

Peter Senge coined the term *creative tension* (1990) to indicate how a group feels when it experiences the gap between where it is and where it wants to go. Creative tension underpins all change work. Without the gap "there would be no need for any action to move toward a vision. Indeed, the gap is *the* source of creative energy" (Senge, 1990, p. 150). In a group process, creative tension is what the group experiences when it becomes aware of the

NEW DIRECTIONS FOR EVALUATION • DOI: 10.1002/ev

gap between where it is and where it wants to go. The tension can be a result of a shared opinion, feeling, or perception (if the group has a shared vision), or a composite of individual opinions, feelings, or perceptions. It is easy to understand the creative tensions present in the evaluation process. Even when stakeholders have a shared mission on paper (although often they don't), they may have different visions for themselves, their community, or their project.

Emotional tension is the mixture of anxiety, worry, and concern that accumulates for those who recognize creative tension (Senge, 1990). Being a skilled and effective facilitator entails being aware of the creative tension without becoming overwhelmed by the emotional tension, while helping participants manage their own emotional tension so that fear doesn't drive the process. If fear is in the driver's seat, participants may give up the vision for more practical goals. Fear can sabotage the group's ability to fulfill its own purpose.

The term *dynamic tension* originates from the combination of the concepts of *creative tension* and *polarity* in organizational development and management. Polarities are opposites that are wrongly approached as problems to be solved. In actuality, they are dilemmas to be managed. Both sides are essential to the well-being of the organization, and choosing one pole over the other doesn't generate a solution but exasperates the imbalance (Johnson, 1992). As an example, consider the process of managing an evaluation project. What's best, structure and planning, or flexibility and adaptability? Based on an evaluator's comfort zone one may lean toward planning more (the first pole) or adapting in the moment more (the second pole). While there are obvious strengths in each pole, there are also downsides. Even intuitively, we know that if one stays rigidly on either pole, the evaluation will suffer. Both sides are indispensable to an effective, relevant, and well-managed evaluation. The polarity is best managed when one is aware of the strengths *and* weaknesses of each pole. An effective facilitator capitalizes on the strengths while keeping an eye on the weaknesses.

Foundation: Definition of Facilitation

For the purpose of this discussion, I'm defining *facilitation* as the art of surfacing, stimulating, and honing the creative tension within a group to help it move where it wants to go, needs to go, and how it wants to go. The *where* can be determined by the group jointly or in the way individual perspectives coalesce or oppose each other once the group interacts. The *how* can also be defined by the group jointly or interactively. To leverage and hone the creative tension, the facilitator must engage and welcome the dynamic tensions in the group.

For facilitators to leverage the energy of a group's creative tension, they need to recognize the dynamic tensions that are present. This means welcoming both opposites or poles and encouraging participants to allow them to coexist and be expressed by resisting the temptation to elevate one side as "right" over the other. By allowing the opposites to coexist, the creative energy between them is released. The facilitator cannot control the moment in which this release takes place, but she or he must trust that it may occur, which it often does. In practical terms, the "release" is often expressed in the finding of a third way, an innovative idea that is not a compromise but a coalescing or a creative solution that energizes the promoters of both sides, generating a shared sense of belonging and accomplishment that propels the process even further.

There are multiple schools of facilitation: Appreciative Inquiry, Deep Democracy, PeerSpirit Circle, Dynamic Facilitation, World Cafe, and so on. Each has its own purpose, philosophy, methodology, and area of practice. In this chapter, I will use the lens of the Art of Hosting meaningful conversations (AOH), a community of facilitation that is especially effective in engaging issues of social complexity, because honing and engaging the creative power of group tensions are at its core. AOH is "an approach to leadership that scales up from the personal to the systemic using personal practice, dialogue, facilitation and the co-creation of innovation to address complex challenges" (www.artofhosting.org). While AOH uses this philosophy and practice of facilitation for the duration of its events whether they last hours or days, the practice of this type of facilitation has much to teach evaluators even if used for a much more limited time frame within a much broader evaluation context. In fact, it can help us prepare for the moments in which even our well-planned meetings may veer out of control. AOH, in fact, highlights the creative role of chaotic moments and the need to learn to create the conditions for a conversation to occur instead of controlling the conversation itself.

Dynamic Tensions for Evaluators Who Facilitate

Dynamic tensions in social settings can make facilitation much harder, so balancing or managing the tension is fundamental to competent facilitation. I've identified seven dynamic tensions that are most relevant for evaluators who facilitate.

Hosting Self ← → Hosting Others

In the Art of Hosting facilitation tradition, hosting self and hosting others are two components of the fourfold practice.[1] *Hosting self* means being present to oneself and to one's own values, priorities, feelings, and needs. It means not subduing our needs to those of the group, but holding a heartfelt

---

[1] These two practices in the fourfold practice work alongside the other two practices: being hosted and being part of a hosting community. The latter two are not included more in depth here because they are not as applicable to evaluation work. See this one-page visual for more: http://uccommunity.org.au/sites/default/files/four_fold_practice_03-13.pdf

presence to ourselves while we are in a group setting. For a facilitator, that may be as simple as pausing for a glass of water when needed, or as difficult as having awareness of how the behavior of a group member is affecting us personally.

Hosting others entails behaving in a way that fosters the comfort of participants, meaningful contributions, and collective intelligence. We sometimes underestimate the role a facilitator plays in setting the tone of the meeting. Chair arrangement, body language, word choice, tone of voice, and the presence of handouts send cues to participants about how open, formal, fun, and even genuine a meeting space will be. As Holman (2010) states, setting a clear intention that energizes the head and the heart is an important aspect of being a host. Setting a clear intention can be even more powerful. While a goal has to be quantifiable, specific, and lead to outcomes, an intention can be a general shared direction that incorporates something more: people being present and aware of their collective purpose. With a clear intention, a group may not get as far as they intended to go at one meeting, but may, in some circumstances, go farther overall. The intention can guide a group to change the process without veering off track, by inspiring new possibilities while tending to the needs of its members and while addressing unpredictable issues that emerge.

To host self and others, you may consider:

- Taking 10 minutes before facilitating, to "check in with" your body, mind, and heart and with any colleagues with whom you are facilitating. Take the time to say something encouraging to yourself and each other.
- Paying special attention to (or role-playing) the first 15 minutes of your meeting. Set the tone for the rest of your time together. Become aware of the routine you follow at home to help guests feel welcomed. Find a routine that works for you professionally—one that is warm and engaging and that says not only that you are competent, but also that you care.

Hosting Stakeholders in the Meeting ← → Hosting Stakeholders Not Present in the Meeting

Different stakeholders have different needs. A skillful facilitator plans conversations so that people with less formal power can give feedback in a protected setting. Delicate information is best shared in pairs rather than in front of a large group, for instance. It is the facilitator's role to plan for a meeting by taking into account how differences among stakeholders may play out in real life. Evaluators can also play a key transformative role in the organization by supporting inclusion and engaging project/program stakeholders in conversations about voices that are not represented (Mertens, 2009). These conversations must be handled in a timely and tactful way and are essential to identifying systemic power dynamics and alternate perspectives. Williams and Hummelbrunner (2011, pp. 16–28) explain systems thinking in seeing the system as the "elements that make up the whole," the "interrelationships that hold the parts together," and the boundaries that determine "what is inside and outside the system." Perspectives of stakeholders who are not generally invited to contribute can provide meaningful insights and solutions.

To host both stakeholders in the meeting and outside the meeting, you may consider:

- Asking yourself ahead of time for each activity or conversation, *Would someone feel uncomfortable doing this? What can I do to increase their comfort level?* Make accommodations for differences in power, learning styles, ages, and personalities. Assess whether you need small-group discussions or large ones, silent journaling or conversations out loud, visuals or lecturing, and a change of seating to stir up a static atmosphere.
- Having a conversation with your client before you facilitate about power dynamics among stakeholders. You could say: *You know, in any meeting, there are always dynamics born from a shared history that I don't know about because I'm not part of your group. Those dynamics can affect what happens during the meeting. The more I know ahead of time, the easier it is for me to be prepared. Can you help me by talking, confidentially, about what subgroups are present? Who was and wasn't invited to the meeting and why? Could I talk with anyone else to get a different perspective?*

Observing Group Dynamics ← → Observing Individual Dynamics

In facilitation, as in management, seeing the forest *and* the trees is essential (Senge, 1990). From systems theory, we understand that the whole is bigger than the sum of the parts and that the way each person or stakeholder group makes meaning of a given situation is different (Williams & Hummelbrunner, 2011). The boundaries that the system sets are rooted in how the situation is being framed, or interpreted. The way a person perceives a situation is dependent upon the power distribution throughout the system and his or her experience with it. For an evaluator, it is important to discern individual interpretations and dynamics from group or subgroup dynamics even when they are implicit. To help a group reflect on a situation, a facilitator might choose to name a boundary to bring attention to it, or reframe it, by offering a new interpretation of a situation that is affected by it.

To help you observe both individual and group dynamics, you may consider:

- Checking in during breaks with your cofacilitator (or journaling) about what you plan next. Ask yourselves, does this still seem the right way to go based on where the group is? Should any modifications be made? Are there any hidden dynamics or findings that need to be named? Any perspectives that need to be reframed?

- Sitting with your cofacilitator (or journaling) during breaks, and making a quick checklist of memorable moments. You might consider asking, what did people say that you remember? What does that say about the relationships between different members? How do individual differences such as race, gender, ethnicity, class, or sexual orientation play out in this group setting?

Simplifying ← → Unveiling Complexity

Simplifying means identifying "the least we need to do to create the most benefit" (Holman, 2010, p. 143). As evaluators, we often do this when we facilitate collective sessions to formulate indicators or identify an evaluation focus. It is also important to allow space for complexity when needed. As complexity theory emphasizes (Cognitive Edge, 2010; Snowden & Boone, 2007), the intellectual, emotional, spiritual, and psychological realms of individuals are complex, where many factors come into play and the results are not predictable. When evaluators build logic models and indicators, we often are doing our best to simplify complex arenas, which at best allows us to revise the tools we generate, but can also have its risks. In Snowden's Cynefin framework, he highlights that trying to force simple frameworks upon complex arenas risks "falling off the cliff" and generating chaos. This is the main reason why complexity theory proposes handling complex situations in different ways rather than simplification. Unveiling complexity means welcoming voices of disturbance and disruption (Holman, 2010). For evaluators who facilitate, this set of practices is useful because it can help us prepare for the unpredictable circumstances that are integral to our work. Welcoming the complexity of a group or organization can help us adapt to changing situations, listen for contextual factors, identify latent variables, and acknowledge blind spots and ignored issues already present. Further, these practices can help us engage and include in our evaluations the internal power differences and structural constraints that stakeholders interact with on a daily basis. It is critical to know when to allow complexity its place and when to simplify. In a meeting to identify indicators, if we simplify too much, we can end up silencing stakeholders who do not see themselves recognized in the measures that are a priority for the selected few.

To practice simplifying interventions while creating space for complexity and disruptive voices, you may consider:

- Asking yourself after you've completed your first draft of planning, *What is the least we can do to create the most benefit? What jargon is familiar to me that is not essential to help others understand me?*

NEW DIRECTIONS FOR EVALUATION • DOI: 10.1002/ev

- When someone disrupts while facilitating, resist the temptation to push them immediately back on track and wait to see how other people in the group respond. Watch if the disturbance gets traction and take a note of it. If or when you have to get participants back on track, try to find the wisdom in the dissenting voice and try to find a place to integrate it into another step in your process.

Listening for What Is ← → Sensing and Fostering Emergence

Emergence is a common term used among facilitators who work in conditions of complexity when the patterns of interactions or solutions are not yet clear and the collective forces are stirring within a group. "Emergence is order arising out of chaos" (Holman, 2010, p. ix). The literature on emergent processes in facilitation is vast and growing (Holman, 2010; Scharmer, 2007). Developmental Evaluation was designed to assist in these processes (Patton, 2010). Most evaluators have had experiences where even a well-planned meeting goes differently than expected and has moments that resemble chaos, where eventually the group manages to make progress through conversation and clarification. *Sensing* is an essential skill to engage emergence (Scharmer, 2007). Sensing means listening at a deeper level to that which is happening beneath the surface. To sense, one must understand what people say about their reality, while paying attention to the underlying perceptions that created that reality. At the same time, a powerful conversation can shift people's underlying perceptions and as a result, the future possibilities also shift. Sensing means paying attention to the transformation that is occurring within the group and the new possibilities that are slowly emerging. Of all dynamic tensions, this can be one of the hardest to master and is best done with a colleague. The person leading the activity can listen to participants' surface reactions, while the colleague who is not implementing the activity is focused on sensing the undercurrent of the conversation. Silent observation is helpful to sensing effectively. The more pragmatic among us can think of it as stepping back and identifying the unspoken common need of a group or recognizing the elephant in the room.

To practice staying in tune both with what is and what is emerging, you may consider:

- Practicing how to remember what people say in a meeting the way you would conduct an observation. Notice first what is occurring without judgment. To help you with this, you can seek additional training in recognizing group dynamics.
- Planning for space and time to sense what is happening at a deeper level. To do this, you need space for being quiet with the group. You may decide to have a cofacilitator or plan activities so that you have some pauses to watch the whole room and simply be present. While your participants

engage in an activity, try sitting or standing at the center and taking deep breaths. Notice how it feels to be in the group. A regular meditation practice can also help you sense at a deeper level.

Intuition-Heart ← → Rational Problem Solving

In the fields of facilitation, leadership development, management, and organizational development, there has recently been a growing appreciation of the role of "heart," emotion, and intuition. There is no doubt that some distance is important for a level-headed perspective, especially in moments of confusion, tension, or outright conflict, but rational problem solving in those moments is not always best. An "open heart" is essential, holding compassion for participants who are absorbed by their own perspectives. Further, intuition can be the most reliable tool, because our subconscious minds handle intuitively and quite spontaneously a plethora of daily physical tasks that are actually quite complex (Holman, 2010; Senge, 1990). This is one of the reasons working with a partner is recommended. When someone with a similar skill set cofacilitates, it is quite easy to check our intuitions and feelings and make the best choice for the group.

To practice using your intuition, heart, and your problem-solving skills, you may consider several options:

- When faced with the choice of which skill set to use, refer to the Cynefin framework, which uses Simple/Complicated/Complex/Chaotic to categorize situations, to identify what kind of situation you're in. If you're in a simple or complicated situation, problem-solve based on your prior experience. If you are in a complex situation, try empathizing with the current disruptive forces. In complex and chaotic situations, try using your intuition (commonly called a *hunch* or your *gut*) to identify new possibilities or processes to get through the crisis. Through it all, hold a tender heart toward yourself. Facilitating through chaos and complexity is not easy!

Chaos ← → Control

Some of the dynamic tensions above can be explained via the chaos-control continuum. There is an underlying dynamic tension between chaos and order in each group setting. As facilitators, our personalities and circumstances may carry both of these tendencies or we may be drawn to one over the other. Each characteristic can be constructive or destructive according to how it's used. A facilitator with a strong chaos drive may help a group uncover submerged conflicts and steer it toward innovative decisions or experiences. This may, however, sow conflict to the point that the group cannot move beyond it. A facilitator with a strong order drive may help restore peace and consensus in a conflict-filled conversation, but may also stifle growth by not challenging the group outside of its comfort zone. It's best to partner with colleagues of different leanings in the awareness that both order and chaos are needed for the best, innovative, collective results to emerge. It can allow us to walk the *chaordic path*—the path that emerges when chaos and order overlap (Hock, 1999). The chaordic path recalls Senge's creative tension as the source of all change.

To learn to dance effectively with chaos and order, you may consider:

- Increasing your awareness of whether you lean toward chaos or order in group dynamics. Start by observing how you interact in groups in your personal life and the effect that your comments or actions have. Then try challenging yourself to act outside of your comfort zone. If you tend to try to calm conflicts, try offering your perspective boldly. If you tend to start controversies, step back and learn how to listen. When you are ready, try intervening based on what you sense the group needs instead of your usual comfort zone actions. Keep a journal to notice changes. Practice in your personal settings before moving to your professional settings.
- Partnering with a colleague in professional settings who has an opposite tendency from your own. Preparing for the event by listing what group dynamics to expect and what conflict could be destructive or constructive. Set an intention with your partner not to avoid tension, but to use your partnership to leverage it at the service of the group.

Role of Self-Reflective Practice

Mastering dynamic tensions takes time, patience, and not only practice, but self-reflective practice. Below are a few questions to help guide self-reflection after each facilitated session:

- Which of the above dynamic tensions was I most aware of in this session? Did I make choices based on my own comfort zone or on the group's needs?
- Did I offer stakeholders enough freedom to express their own evaluation questions, concerns, or priorities? Did all stakeholders speak up? How can I create an opportunity to hear their perspectives?
- What was hardest for me to implement while listening deeply? How can I plan ahead or get further support in the future to make up for this?
- In setting priorities, did I listen enough to hear stakeholders' concerns before making choices or did I prioritize what I considered practical, operationable, or evaluable?
- Where was I bold? Where did I step back and sense-in? Which best served the group? Did I get in the way of the group process?

- For which activities is it easiest for me to play an implementer role, a listening role, or a harvesting[2] role? Should I work on strengthening those areas or delegate to others?
- What roles did my partner or team members and I take on? Should we distribute roles differently next time? Did my team members and I complement each other well, or did we crowd the room because of overlapping strengths? Did I play more of a chaos or order role in this event? Was it to the best service of the group?

To enhance reflective practice, one may consider attending a 5-day Group Relations conference by the Rice Institute (www.akrice.org). Through a psychoanalytic approach to group dynamics, one learns how one's personality affects group interactions.

Implications

Considering the breadth and depth of skills needed to facilitate effectively, it is no surprise that facilitation requires ongoing learning. The skills mentioned above can help an evaluator who facilitates leverage his or her leadership skills at the service of the group. As of now, there is little focus in the literature on how to assess or self-assess when these skills are being used effectively. As evaluators, our skill set can be helpful to the field for creating processes and tools that help improve these in-the-moment practices, as well as documenting how and when the skill set is being implemented most effectively. Increased attention to these areas is relevant to improving our practice both as facilitators and evaluators.

References

Cognitive Edge. (July 2010). *The Cynefin Framework* [Video file]. Retrieved from https://www.youtube.com/watch?v=N7oz366X0-8

Hock, D. (1999). *Birth of the chaordic age.* San Francisco, CA: Berrett-Koehler.

Holman, P. (2010). *Engaging emergence: Turning upheaval into opportunity.* San Francisco, CA: Berrett-Koehler.

Johnson, B. (1992). *Polarity management: Identifying and managing unsolvable problems.* Amherst, MA: HRD.

Mertens, D. M. (2009). *Transformative research and evaluation.* New York, NY: Guilford Press.

Patton, M. K. (2010). *Developmental evaluation: Applying complexity concepts to enhance innovation and use.* New York, NY: Guilford Press.

Scharmer, C. O. (2007). *Theory U: Leading from the future as it emerges.* Cambridge, MA: Sarthe Society for Organizational Learning.

Senge, P. M. (1990). *The fifth discipline: The art and practice of the learning organization.* London, UK: Random House.

---

[2]The term *harvesting* is used in the Art of Hosting community to indicate the planned and purposeful documentation of meetings and event content, themes, and processes.

NEW DIRECTIONS FOR EVALUATION • DOI: 10.1002/ev

Snowden, D. J., & Boone, M. (2007). A leader's framework for decision making. *Harvard Business Review*, 85, 69–76.
Williams, B., & Hummelbrunner, R. (2011). *Systems concepts in action*. Stanford, CA: Stanford University Press.

RITA S. FIERRO, PhD, is the founder of Fierro Consulting, LLC, a firm working for national and international organizations, nonprofits, foundations, and innovative businesses in North America, Europe, New Zealand, and Africa that uses facilitation, evaluation, and research to help inspire individuals, groups, and communities to thrive in excellence while they pursue their goals together. You can find out more about her work from her website: www.fierroconsultingllc.com.

NEW DIRECTIONS FOR EVALUATION • DOI: 10.1002/ev

Pipi, K. (2016). MĀRAMATANGA (enlightenment): A creative approach to connecting facilitation and evaluation. In R. S. Fierro, A. Schwartz, & D. H. Smart (Eds.), *Evaluation and
Facilitation. New Directions for Evaluation, 149*, 43–52.

3

MĀRAMATANGA (Enlightenment): A Creative Approach to Connecting Facilitation and Evaluation

Kataraina Pipi

Abstract

*This paper presents a personal narrative from an indigenous practitioner who
uses creative facilitation methods as part of her evaluation work. The narrative
describes examples of tools used in facilitation and evaluation, along with some
of the lessons learned from integrating creativity and structured processes when
working with indigenous people in Aotearoa (New Zealand). These lessons include that it is important to facilitate critical reflection from a cultural base; that
through culturally grounded facilitation, evaluation can come to have meaning
in culturally specific ways; and that creativity is what links facilitation and
evaluation.* © 2016 Wiley Periodicals, Inc., and the American Evaluation
Association.

I have 25 years of experience in facilitation, music, and evaluation in
Aotearoa (New Zealand). My approach to these three interwoven dimensions of my working life reflects who I am as a Māori woman, a
mother, a facilitator, an evaluator, and a musician. When these elements
are combined, I find I am the most able to support the realization of indigenous aspirations. My practice has emerged over time but has always

involved the use of collaborative group activities and experiences that seek to engage people at many different levels: through memories, emotions, stories, and exploring ways of being and knowing through different cultural worldviews. Using a combination of facilitative, evaluative, creative, and cultural methods, I encourage and support people to talk, listen, reflect, feel, and remember. By deliberately prompting deep insights into what matters, and allowing for personal and collective contributions in cultural terms, I am able to affirm who people are and what is important to them.

My definition of facilitation is a process that enables individuals and group participants to "journey with ease from point A to point B." It is my belief that there is a deep connection between facilitation and evaluation. In my experience, sound facilitation skills and experience can be the difference between poor and high-quality information and evaluation. Indigenous evaluation requires genuine engagement with communities, facilitated discussions of substance, and culturally responsive critical reflection about what works for indigenous peoples (Cram, Kennedy, Paipa, Pipi, & Wehipeihana, in press). This enables initiatives to be assessed and represented within evaluation reports in ways that assure empowering processes and outcomes for communities. The following insights are provided from a practitioner perspective. They are drawn from my experience working in, and with, Māori communities. These are communities where people love to sing, share stories, learn and reflect together, and see themselves in a positive light. It is my job to work with and, if I am able, to enhance these characteristics and values.

The remainder of this introduction describes my entry into evaluation. I then provide an illustration of how I combine facilitation, evaluation, and creativity within my practice, before I describe some of the tools I use.

My Entry Into Evaluation

I am a composer/musician and enjoy singing and sharing stories through songs, for healing, for pleasure, and as a way of retelling our history as *tangata whenua* (meaning "people of the land"). I was a facilitator before I became involved in evaluation. I trained in neuro-linguistic programming (NLP), am a certified TetraMap facilitator and a PATH facilitator and trainer. NLP provides a way of understanding the connection between the mind, emotions, language, and behavior. NLP training gave me an in-depth appreciation of a wide range of strategies that can be applied in personal development, business, and community development. TetraMap is a behavioral model based on the elements of nature (earth, air, water, fire) that can help simplify the complex and provide a framework that is helpful in exploring human behavior (Brett & Brett, 2007). PATH is a visual planning tool used to support individuals, groups, and communities to visualize a positive and possible future and is discussed later in this chapter. The combination of

NEW DIRECTIONS FOR EVALUATION • DOI: 10.1002/ev

these tools has contributed to my own unique style of facilitation within indigenous communities.

I began my research and evaluation career in 2000 when I had the opportunity to work on an exciting piece of research alongside Dr. Fiona Cram, the Iwi and Māori Provider Success Research project (Pipi et al., 2003). Since then, I have had the privilege of working alongside some wonderful Māori and non-Māori researchers and evaluators and have enjoyed the opportunity to combine my musical interests, facilitation skills, and evaluation.

My pathway into evaluation has happened in a decade where there have been some stimulating developments for Māori and indigenous evaluation in Aotearoa. These developments have provided an important context for my own practice development. They include: an overall increase in the number of Māori evaluators, an increase in Māori evaluators completing postgraduate studies in evaluation, and a mostly shared vision in the wider evaluation community about the value of "by Māori, for Māori" evaluation approaches, with Māori evaluators now leading many evaluation projects within Māori communities. There has also been active involvement of Māori evaluators in the Aotearoa New Zealand Evaluation Association (www.anzea.org.nz). The association has a Māori evaluation development strategy, as well as evaluator competencies and evaluation standards projects that have Māori leading and determining the Māori focus of these projects.

The impact of these developments on my own experience and practice is that my personal sense of responsibility to contribute to the growing body of knowledge around *kaupapa Maori* (by Māori, for Māori) research and evaluation is heightened. In addition, the value of the skill of facilitation when engaging in our communities to elicit culturally specific information becomes more necessary.

Combining Facilitation, Evaluation, and Music

This section provides an example that illustrates the usefulness of combining facilitation, evaluation, and creativity through music composition when engaging with communities. It illustrates three key learnings about what can occur when combining these three aspects.

Recently I had the honor of traveling to the Chatham Islands, off the east coast of Aotearoa, as part of an action research team. We visited the local Māori community service provider; our task was to learn about who they were, what their philosophy was, and hear of their journey to date supporting *whānau* ("family") and community aspirations. My first thoughts were about how best to facilitate a mutual learning process, in which the action research team could learn about the community, and the community could learn about action research and how it might be of value to them. I turned to music and facilitated a songwriting session where everyone in the group shared some words about who they are and what is important to them. The words included concepts that they collectively identified, such as valuing family, place, community, and cultural connections.

Those of us in the action research team then shared that we wanted to work together with them, to walk alongside and reflect with them as critical friends.

Out of this discussion, the acronym PAORA was formed from the words: plan, act, observe, reflect, and anō ("do it all over again"). Paora is a translation of the name Paul, which many would know. Being able to use words and meanings that resonate culturally really helped the community understand what action research was all about in a simple and memorable way. Once we had our "lyrics" (made up of our collective words of meaning), I put a tune to the song, and within an hour we were singing a song that captured the way action research would be utilized with the community of the Chatham Islands.

Throughout the process of composing the song, there were moments where we veered off and dug a little deeper into aspects of what we were singing about. We decided that the song would be in the Māori language, even though there were a number of people present who had minimal understanding of the language. Engaging in deep reflection about the words of the song was insightful and affirming for these participants.

We had been working on another evaluation at the time, and I shared with the group the *kaupapa* (purpose) of the program that was called *Kia Rite, Kia Ora* ("Preparing for Living a Healthy Life"). This was a diabetes self-management program that was run by Whaiora Trust in Masterton, Aotearoa. They liked the concept of *kia rite* ("getting ready"), *kia ora* ("for good health") and thought that those words aptly described what they were about to embark on for their Whānau Ora ("well-being of the family") and action research journey (Cram, 2011).

We talked about the philosophy and approach to their work with *whanau*, or "family," in the Chathams and their intent to ensure that they met the needs of the range of *whānau* who came to their service. They used the analogy of the *harakeke* ("flax bush") and described their intent to regenerate the *pā harakeke*, the "flax plantation," on the island in order that *whānau* are protected and cared for. So we sought to weave their values into the song so that it inspired and motivated them toward their dreams of serving their people well.

This experience illustrates three key points of *kaupapa Māori* or "by Māori, for Māori" research and evaluation. First, it is important to facilitate critical reflection from a cultural base, as often everything Māori do is filtered through our senses, including *maumahara* ("remembering; a sense that comes from past memories"). I always make a conscious effort to "put the Māori mirror up" in front of people and have them reflect on their worldview, their values, their progress, and their achievements through

Māori eyes. Dr. Ani Mikaere, Director of Maori Laws and Philosophy at Te Wānanga-o-Raukawa (a tribal university in the lower North Island) provides an explanation of the value of a Māori worldview:

> There is no doubt that the worldview bequeathed to us by our ancestors lies at the very heart of what makes us unique. It provides the lens through which we view the world. It determines the way in which we relate to one another and to all other facets of creation. It enables us to explain how we came to be here and where we are going. It forms the very core of our identity. (Mikaere, 2011, pp. 307–308)

Second, through culturally grounded facilitation, research and evaluation can come to have meaning in culturally specific ways for Māori communities. This increases the likelihood of community engagement and participation in evaluative thinking and practice and ultimately ensures the overall validity of evaluation (Kirkhart, 2005).

And finally, I have found that in my practice creativity is what links facilitation and evaluation, whether this happens through the use of drawing, music, storytelling, drama, or other artistic pursuits. Drawing is a thinking tool and a medium for making meaning (Agerbeck, 2012). It is the creative part that is the glue for linking insight, reflection, learning, and understanding.

Since the first visit, I have had opportunity to continue my work in the Chatham Islands working with families and the community supporting their development. The next section outlines a series of tools that I successfully used in the Chatham Islands and believe could be useful in other indigenous communities and indeed any communities.

Tools that Combine Facilitation, Evaluation, and Creativity

There are three particular tools I use extensively that combine facilitation, evaluation, and creativity. They are (1) the PATH planning tool; (2) an exercise called SES that is a critical reflection exercise; and (3) graphic facilitation.

PATH: Planning Alternative Tomorrows With Hope

I first discovered the PATH planning tool while on an overseas visit in 2000 to Ma Mawi Chi Itata (an aboriginal-based social services organization) in Winnipeg, Canada. PATH is a visual tool that uses pictures, colors, and symbols to reflect dreams, aspirations, goals, and plans. Through PATH facilitation, we see how visual representation supports discussion, reflection, and affirmation of thoughts and ideas. As a facilitator, I am always

NEW DIRECTIONS FOR EVALUATION • DOI: 10.1002/ev

on the lookout for new tools, and I was impressed with the visual nature of the tool and asked for information about it. I made contact with one of the creators of the tool, Jack Pearpoint from Inclusion Press, Toronto, and he has since supported the use of PATH in my facilitation and evaluation work in Aotearoa.

The PATH planning tool helps individuals, groups, businesses, and *whānau* or "families" reflect upon where they are in terms of their current goals and dreams, their uniqueness, attributes and strengths, and their aspirations for the future (Pipi, 2010). I use PATH extensively in any form of planning work, train PATH facilitators, and am currently focusing on the use of PATH as a tool to support *whānau* planning.

When facilitating the process, a number of questions are asked of participants at each stage, many of which are evaluative questions such as: What are your goals? What specific measures will indicate successful achievement of the outcomes? Where are you now compared to where you want to be in the future? To what extent have you already progressed any of your goals?

An evaluation (Moss, Smith, Spee, & King, 2012) was undertaken of the PATH facilitator training course and PATH planning work with families that I have led in the Chatham Islands. The findings from the evaluation supported my own assertions about the value of PATH. As part of this evaluation, there was a focus on the potential use of PATH as an evaluative tool. I was asked to explain how I have used aspects of PATH in my evaluation work. Facilitating a PATH is a huge data-collection exercise—finding out what people's aspirations, dreams and visions are, where they are now, where they want to be in 5 years, what their values are, and what might prevent them from achieving their goals, and so on.

SES: Success, Evidence, Strategies

SES is an exercise that I developed to support critical reflection, affirmation, and validation. We have used this tool in a range of contexts including personal planning, strategic planning, team building, and evaluation. It is used to help individuals, groups, or businesses identify and become more conscious of what success is, how they measure it and what strategies they use for achieving it. The exercise is particularly powerful in a Māori context, as it supports the unpacking of inherent cultural knowledge, wisdom, and experience in a way that supports understanding and critical reflection. It works well in a situation such as strategic planning where it is framed as a critical reflection on past activities to inform future planning and decision making.

This exercise brings together my knowledge, experience, and skills in the areas of evaluation, facilitation, and cultural competence. It first emerged as part of a research project that I worked on alongside Dr. Fiona

Cram in the year 2000, which looked at the determinants of Māori provider success, where 60 Māori and *Iwi* (meaning, "tribal") providers from a range of sectors, including health, social services, justice, and housing, were invited to participate in a research project that had them identifying why they were successful.

In this project, we facilitated a process of "unpacking how providers do success," and then gathered evidence to substantiate their success. Essential to this was identifying the cultural factors that contribute to success. Many of the participants reflected on how they are in their "cultural skin" and why they do the things they do from a cultural perspective. This meant unpacking what they do as Māori, as *Ngāti Porou* (a tribal group from the east coast of the North Island), and from their cultural, tribal, and *whānau* or "family" knowledge base.

The activity involves participants identifying their three greatest achievements within a given time period. The number *three* is significant because we are seeking to identify the patterns of thinking and behavior, and this requires more than one example to determine. These might be an event, a milestone, or an outcome. For each event or achievement, they are invited to identify the evidence of that success. Evidence is explained as what we can see, hear, feel, and what the facts are, that tell us this has indeed been a success. Participants are then asked to consider the strategies they used to achieve the success. Prompts are given to encourage them to think of these strategies from a number of different angles, such as evaluation, culture, and innovation. The SES exercise provides an example of reflecting on the success of a program in an evaluation context (see Table 3.1). A range of evidence is identified, such as support from elders and the use of a cultural framework.

Table 3.1. Success, Evidence, Strategies Example

Context	Success	Evidence	Strategies
Evaluation	The success of a program	Program statistics (showing positive outcomes) Increases in numbers of young people on the program Descriptives of the young people engaged Support from the elders The cultural framework's acceptance and endorsement by communities	Development of the outcomes framework and data collection system The use of young people from different cultures who speak their native tongue The elders advisory group Innovation: embedding culture within the program

Individuals and families on the Chatham Islands found this exercise to be very affirming. Many had never stopped to reflect on their achievements and they felt very supported as a result. This gave them hope for the achievement of future goals.

Graphic Recording: A Tool for Visual Anchoring

Many of our people (Māori) are visual learners, which may come from the traditional use of graphic tools such as *whakairo* (meaning, "carving") and *tukutuku* (meaning, "lattice work") to pass on knowledge. The art of graphic facilitation has been strengthened for me through my use of the PATH planning tool. In Māori communities, the use of graphic recording, using cultural symbols and language specific to participants, is a powerful way of grounding the work we do in our own worldview, again affirming and validating Māori knowledge and experience.

I call myself a "Flipchart Queen" because in every facilitation I do I use flipcharts to ensure there is a graphic record of all deliberations. This serves a number of purposes. Unlike the PowerPoint slide, which is visible one moment and gone the next, flipchart records can keep the information visually accessible throughout the entire session. Flipchart graphic recording can be a tool for visual anchoring of key information. An image with color can serve as an anchor to a concept, idea, or key information, and this aids memory retention.

I have used graphic recording as a way of visually presenting evaluation findings, telling the story of the journey of a program, including processes and outcomes. We also use graphics to frame and anchor discussion in particular ways. For example, if in a group we are reflecting and discussing learning or education, the graphic often used is a *kete* (meaning, "flax-woven basket"). A *kete* is symbolic of "baskets of knowledge" and often referred to when talking about learning in Māori culture. The flax symbol was used often in our work on the Chatham Islands where flax grows in abundance and is an important reminder for Māori of their resilience, strength, and ability to weave together ideas and activities in this remote setting.

Sometimes the representation of information in a visual form also provokes new insights and learning from different perspectives. An example of this is in an evaluation of a Māori leadership training program. On the last day of the course, we facilitated an evaluation session that asked participants to think back to where they were before the training and where they are now, and to consider what changed directly as a result of their participation in the training.

The method we used was to invite participants to draw a "before" and "after" picture followed by a "once upon a time" story that describes the two pictures. This is a creative approach to critical reflection of a journey. Figure 3.1 shows an example of this where the participant drew a picture

Figure 3.1. A Visual Graphic and Story of Pre- and Posttraining Program Reflections

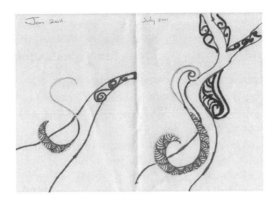

that encapsulated his journey from the beginning of participating in a training program (January 2011) to the end (July 2011) with the story that explains the graphic.

January 2011

The S is me on my journey. The pathway is my work. I am aware of the restructuring in my organization, which will leave me without a job. The *koru* (meaning, "spiral design") at the end of the pathway represents working with Māori, which is a priority for me. The pattern on the S represents the knowledge and confidence I have in *Whanau Ora* (meaning, "a healthy focus on family"). At the beginning of the course, I felt a little intimidated by the knowledge and experience of the other participants. Many were managers and leaders already. I felt a bit out of my depth.

July 2011

The S is bigger. I feel more confident about what I have to offer and what has been given to me. The pathway has a bend in it because, during the recent months, the restructuring was finalized and my job got an ending date. The pathway has options at the end now, and one path has *korus* or "spirals" on the inside representing working for Māori in a Māori organization, and the other has the *koru* on the outside representing working for Māori in a generic/mainstream organization. I feel more equipped to do any work. The *koru* and design in the bend represent the support from the Titoko o te Ao (program name) group. The pattern has grown and extends to the top; however, there is plenty of room for continued growth. *Mauri Ora* (meaning "good health to all")!

In my experience, when creativity is used to reflect on learning, it invokes thinking and outcomes that can often differ from those expressed using more traditional methods of gathering information.

Conclusion

The facilitating evaluator or evaluating facilitator must be informed by the worldview and values of their own indigenous people. By utilizing processes such as storytelling or song, new questions and solutions are generated. Participants may be surprised when they experience what was once considered unreachable now being possible.

My practice combines facilitation, creativity, and evaluation, encouraging the generation of new ideas from a synthesis of traditional, current, or contemporary ideas. The tools I use can be adapted for many contexts and purposes, but they all contain elements of each. The combination affirms and validates Māori experience and worldview. As a Māori facilitator, evaluator, and musician, this approach is grounded in who I am.

References

Agerbeck, B. (2012). *The graphic facilitator's guide: How to use your listening, thinking and drawing skills to make meaning.* Retrieved from http://www.Loosetooth.com
Brett, Y., & Brett, J. (2007). *TetraMap—Develop people and business the way nature intended.* Auckland, New Zealand: TetraMap International Limited.
Cram, F. (June, 2011). *Whānau Ora & Action Research. Paper prepared for Te Puni Kōkiri.* Auckland: Katoa Ltd.
Cram, F., Kennedy, V., Paipa, K., Pipi, K., & Wehipeihana, N. (in press). Being culturally responsive through Kaupapa Māori evaluation. In S. Hood, R. Hopson, K. Obeidat, & H. Frierson (Eds.), *Continuing the journey to reposition culture and cultural context in evaluation theory and practice.* Charlotte, NC: Information Age.
Kirkhart, K. E. (2005). Through a cultural lens: Reflections on validity and theory in evaluation. In S. Hood, R. Hopson, & H. Frierson (Eds.), *The role of culture and cultural context: A mandate for inclusion, the discovery of truth, and understanding in evaluative theory and practice* (pp. 21–39). Greenwich, CT: Information Age.
Mikaere, A. (2011). *Colonising myths Māori realities: He rukuruku whakaaro.* Wellington, New Zealand: Huia Publishers and Te Tākupu, Te Wānanga o Raukawa.
Moss, M., Smith, R., Spee, K., & King, J. (2012). *Formative evaluation of PATH facilitation training and PATH Whānau planning.* Wellington, New Zealand: Kinnect Group.
Pipi, K., Cram, F., Hawke, R., Hawke, S., Huriwai, T. M., Mataki, T., . . . Tuuta, C. (2003). *A research ethic for studying Māori and Iwi provider success.* Wellington, New Zealand: Te Puni Kōkiri.
Pipi, K. (2010). The PATH Planning Tool and its potential for whānau research. *MAI Review, 3,* 84–91.

KATARAINA PIPI *is of Ngāti Porou/Ngāti Hine descent, indigenous to Aotearoa/ New Zealand, lives in Auckland, has two children, and her own business in facilitation/evaluation and making Māori music, thus the acronym for the business name—FEM!*

Torres, R. T. (2016). Planning and facilitating working sessions with evaluation stakehold-ers. In R. S. Fierro, A. Schwartz, & D. H. Smart (Eds.), *Evaluation and Facilitation. New Directions for Evaluation, 149*, 53–66.

4

Planning and Facilitating Working Sessions with Evaluation Stakeholders

Rosalie T. Torres

Abstract

Facilitation is the process of bringing together, engaging, and following up with stakeholders resulting in new insights, perspectives, and potential actions, which (a) in all likelihood would have not otherwise occurred and (b) advance the interests of the stakeholder group. The most critical element of a success-fully facilitated working session is the extent to which all potential influences are addressed during a planning phase. The chapter explains 15 interdependent components for successfully facilitated working sessions and includes a case ex-ample that describes the planning, execution, debriefing, and intended follow-up to one session. It concludes by addressing (a) issues that arose in the session and how they related to information that was or was not available during plan-ning and (b) the facilitation approaches/techniques used to address those issues. © 2016 Wiley Periodicals, Inc., and the American Evaluation Association.

W orking sessions are the hallmark of collaborative, participatory evaluation and are especially important in promoting stake-holder engagement in constructivist learning as part of engaging in and learning from evaluation processes, as well as the use of findings. Working sessions with evaluation stakeholders are typically facilitated by one or more persons on an evaluation team. Facilitation is the process of bringing together, engaging, and following up with stakeholders resulting in new insights, perspectives, and potential actions, which (a) in all likelihood would have not otherwise occurred and (b) advance the interests of the stakeholder group.

The most critical element of a successfully facilitated working session is the extent to which all potential influences are addressed during a planning phase (Torres, Preskill, & Piontek, 2001). This chapter identifies those components and influences, highlights relevant facilitation issues, and provides questions and discussion related to each. Extensive planning is important because successfully facilitated working sessions are mentally taxing, requiring facilitators to process and respond in the moment to new information, perspectives, and reactions from the group. Successful facilitation goes far beyond what happens during any one working session. It results from first relating all aspects of the session to its specific objectives.

The chapter also includes a case example that describes the planning, execution, debriefing, and intended follow-up to one session. It concludes by addressing (a) issues that arose in the session and how they related to information that was or was not available during planning and (b) the facilitation approaches/techniques used to address those issues.

Successful facilitators devote considerably more time planning than conducting a session and they learn as they go. This experientially based skill is grounded in well-informed planning and debriefing about successes, challenges, and refinements to strategy and techniques (see Preskill & Torres, 1998). The chapter builds on the work of this author and others who have long advocated the value of well-facilitated working sessions to engage stakeholders in learning on individual, group, and organizational levels (see, e.g., De Coninck, Chaturvedi, Haagsma, Griffioen, & van der Glas, 2008; Patton, 2012; Torres, 2006; Torres & Preskill, 2001; Torres et al., 2005; Torres, Stone, Butkus, Hook, Casey, & Arens, 2000).

Planning for Successfully Facilitated Evaluation Working Sessions

The following section details 15 specific planning components or procedural steps for successful working sessions, from identifying the session's purpose to following up on its outcomes and processes. Although these steps are necessarily presented in a chronological order, the planning process is not linear. Readers are encouraged to review all 15 highly interdependent planning components before beginning with any one.

(1) Purpose: What is the purpose of the working session?

Working sessions can be useful in any aspects of the evaluation where it is important that collaboration and engagement resulting in constructivist learning take place: (a) between the evaluators and stakeholders, and/or (b) among the stakeholders themselves. Consider how working sessions might be helpful to:

NEW DIRECTIONS FOR EVALUATION • DOI: 10.1002/ev

- Identify stakeholders' concerns and conceptualize the evaluation problem.
- Develop and refine the program's theory of action and/or logic model.
- Make decisions about data collection methods and other evaluation activities.
- Engage stakeholders in interpreting data.
- Solicit feedback about initial evaluation findings and/or interpretations developed by the evaluator.
- Develop conclusions, recommendations, and/or specific action plans.
- Be mindful that fully addressing any one of these purposes could take more than one working session. Trying to accomplish too much in one session is a common learning experience for evaluators new to this practice. After identifying key players (Item 3), and in conjunction with your response here, be specific about desired outcomes (Item 6).

(2) Planners: Who else should be involved in the planning of this working session?

How will you solicit their involvement? What aspects of this session are they most likely to inform, be concerned about, and so on? How can engaging particular persons in the planning process help the session be more successful?

(3) Key Players: Which individuals or groups have influence over or will be impacted by the project, the evaluation processes, and/or the use of its results?

More specifically:

- Who can inform the topic, issue, or purpose of the session?
- Who is directly involved or has a vested interest in the topic/issue?
- Who will be affected by the outcomes of this working session?
- Who has a right to be included in this working session?

In many cases, these are the same persons who might be included on an evaluation team with responsibilities for providing input to, engaging in, and using the results of the evaluation. Additional persons might be included in any of the working sessions.

(4) Potential Issues among Key Players: What issues, if any, do you foresee among the individuals/groups you identified attending a single working session on the topic you have chosen?

Consider the following:

- Group size too large.
- Individuals/groups unfamiliar with each other.
- Individuals/groups have highly variant backgrounds or perspectives on topic/issue.

- Individuals/groups are highly diverse (in race/ethnicity/culture, literacy levels, age, etc.).
- Political issues make bringing some individuals/groups together inadvisable or inappropriate.

(5) Number and Grouping of Sessions: Considering your responses to the questions above, might it be necessary to conduct more than one working session on the same topic?

Under any of the circumstances just listed, separate working sessions with different groups might be warranted, with a strategy for building consensus across groups in a subsequent larger meeting. If so, who would attend each session? Or, might it be appropriate to conduct a single working session with representatives of various groups? Deciding who should be included in any one session can be tricky, with success sometimes largely dependent on the evaluator's facilitation skills. Whatever grouping is chosen, unforeseen political issues, conflicts, or tensions may arise during the session. Your skills at giving voice to varying perspectives while reducing possible tension in the group could be called upon.

(6) Specific Outcomes: Considering the foregoing and being as specific as possible, what would you and other key collaborators like to see as outcomes for the session?

Once the overall purpose of the meeting has been established, naming specific objectives may seem redundant. Thinking though a concrete product (e.g., an evaluation plan in full or in part, a revised logic model, a set of conclusions or interpretations, an implementation action plan) can help refine the overall purpose into objectives. Detailing specific objectives will communicate to the group the task at hand and what the meeting is intended to produce (see Exhibit 4.1 of the case study, later on).

(7) Timing: Ideally, when should this working session take place?

Those experienced with using working sessions as part of the evaluation may build them when designing the evaluation (see Torres et al., 2005, Chapter 2). Doing so helps communicate to stakeholders the importance of this kind of collaborative engagement, and establishes the expectation that time will be needed to do so (see Item 1). That being said, working sessions can be undertaken at any time during the evaluation. Finally, is it more important to conduct the meeting only when all can attend or to conduct the meeting by a certain date? If a certain date is more important, how will you follow up with those who may not be able to attend?

(8) Participant Engagement: How will you engage participants during the working session?

Think about how participants will interact with information you will provide, with each other, and with you. What different facilitation methods will you use? In addition to your presenting information, consider the use of worksheets, brainstorming, small group work, focus-group type dialogs,

Exhibit 4.1. Final Working Session Agenda

Evaluation Team Working Session
Date
9 a.m. to 1 p.m.

Session Objectives
(1) Reach consensus on updated version of the logic model
(2) Establish the evaluation priorities
(3) Outline evaluation methods

Agenda
A. Introductions (9:05)
B. Orientation to Session and Agenda Review (9:15)
C. Review of Original Logic Model (9:20)
D. Small Groups: Logic Model Revisions by Project Area (9:40)
E. Break (10:15)
F. Large Group: Small-Group Reporting and Integration of Results (10:25)
G. Development of Evaluation Questions for Each Logic Model Component and Beyond (11:25)
H. Working Lunch and Prioritization of Evaluation Questions (11:55)
I. Data Collection Methods for Priority Evaluation Questions (12:30)
J. Review of Next Steps (12:45)
K. Session Debrief and Closing (12:50)

and so on. Providing a structure helps participants focus on the topic and achieve the objectives of the session. (See Item 10 for more on background information as a starting point for participant engagement.)

(9) Facilitation Skills: What skills do you or other facilitators possess to engage participants in these ways?

Table 4.1 lists three key facilitation skills, along with the rationale, benefits of, and specific details for their use—ranging from deeply understanding where you as the facilitator stand on the topic of the working session to refocusing the session midstream.

(10) Participant Background and Information Needs: What background information should be provided so that all participants have common ground?

A shared understanding of basic information on the session's issues and topics can save time during subsequent dialog by addressing potential questions at the start. Examples include reviewing a previously developed logic model and presenting evaluation findings for subsequent discussion and interpretation. What would be a good way to provide this information? Will you need to include an opportunity for discussion regarding the background information? What's the best way to facilitate that discussion to ensure everyone can take part? Besides an agenda, would it be helpful to send out any information ahead of time? Should the participants come prepared in any particular way?

Table 4.1. Rationale, Benefits, and Specific Details for Using Three Key Facilitation Skills

Key Facilitation Skills	Rationale and Benefits of Use	Specific Details for Use
A. Be aware of your own values, beliefs, and assumptions.	At their best, facilitators are helping others—the evaluation stakeholders—think deeply about their own values, beliefs, and assumptions. Knowing where we ourselves stand is key to not letting any unconscious agendas of our own influence how we guide others in this process.	1. Review and explore your prior experiences with similar projects and stakeholder groups. 2. What do you believe as a result of those experiences? 3. How might these beliefs influence the present evaluation work and how you engage with stakeholders? 4. Would it be helpful to at least temporarily suspend these beliefs?
B. Draw on participants' values, beliefs, assumptions, knowledge, and experience.	Because facilitation is meant to lead individuals and the group as a whole to new perspectives and/or potential actions, it must necessarily engage participants both affectively and cognitively. From this point, new information and perspectives can be considered and potentially modified, sometimes leading to consensus-building on key issues.	1. Assume little to nothing about where stakeholders are coming from. 2. Early in the facilitation process, ask for their input and make it the substance of subsequent activities. 3. In order to reveal underlying values and assumptions, allow time for asking participants what perspectives and experiences influence their input. ("Do you have some prior experience with this issue? Maybe we can learn from you on this.")
C. Be willing and able to refocus or change the agenda as indicated in the moment; and explain how the change relates to the original plan.	Generally speaking, the less familiar the evaluator is with a given project and its stakeholders, the more likely a need to refocus a planned agenda may arise. Facilitators must sometimes engage in a delicate dance between and among: • The planned agenda. • What stakeholders bring to the session. • Extending an activity or transitioning to a new activity, while at the same time not losing focus of the original purpose of the meeting.	Trusting and flowing with the session's process can reveal more than one way to get from planned activities of a working session to its objectives. Consider: 1. Getting input from the group on how to reach the objectives, given a change in activities. 2. Specific follow-up work that can be undertaken by one or more persons. 3. Getting buy-in from the group for additional meeting time as might be needed.

(11) Agenda: Based on your thinking so far, what would a draft agenda to accomplish the outcomes, described in (6), look like?

That is, what will you ask participants to do in order to accomplish the session objectives? Consider:

1. Beginning the substantive work of the session (i.e., following introductions and/or ice-breaker activities) with a review or presentation of background information directly pertinent to the session.
2. Following this didactic engagement with soliciting participant input. Try to think creatively here, going beyond questions and answers.
3. Alternatively, and depending upon the purpose of the session, beginning with an opportunity for participants to voice their perspectives. For example, a session designed to identify stakeholders' concerns and conceptualize the evaluation problem might begin by asking participants to write down their hopes for and biggest concerns about the evaluation. Follow this with two round-robin activities (one for hopes and one for concerns) asking participants to voice one hope and one concern in turn until all the different hopes and concerns within the group have been named. Follow this up with a dialog about the meaning of the two lists.
4. For more focused work and depending on the number of participants, breaking into small groups, followed by reporting out and integrating results across small groups to create new understanding within the group as a whole.
5. Concluding the session with a review of what has been accomplished and a clear set of next steps. Ask participants what they have learned, what insights they have gained, and if appropriate, what actions they are likely to take as a result of their participation.
6. Allowing time for getting feedback on how the session worked.

(12) Time Needed: What's an estimate of the time necessary for this agenda?

This question must also be balanced with the time you feel you can get from the group. Experience strongly suggests that most evaluation working sessions require a bare minimum of 90 minutes, with up to a full day being useful for an extended agenda. A well-facilitated session that starts on time can yield desired (and sometimes unforeseen, but beneficial) outcomes in two hours. The abiding challenge is to find common dates and times when all key players are available for two hours or more.

(13) Next Steps: What are the likely next steps following this meeting to move forward in the evaluation work?

Successful facilitators usually have anticipated a clear next step in the process, such as refining the evaluation plan based on collaborative input and decision making from the group. Considering the session's intended outcomes, what do you anticipate specific next steps will be and what tasks will you and/or others undertake for those steps? However, it is important to hold this step as tentative—ready to be fully shaped and formed based on how the session goes. (See Item 9.)

(14) Logistics: What steps are necessary for you to prepare the presentation of information, activities, worksheets, or handouts that will be a part of this working session? Where might this meeting take place?

What media will be used? Printed documents, posters, flip charts, PowerPoint displays, sticky notes, markers, and so on? (See Item 8.)

Is any advance planning necessary to secure a meeting place? Consider having sufficient room for: viewing presentations; small group, large group, and/or individual work; serving refreshments; accommodating any media that will be used. The less cramped participants are, the better.

(15) Lessons Learned: What can you learn from how the session went and what can you do about what you learned?

No two facilitated working sessions are ever exactly alike. Each has lessons to share. Schedule a time to debrief the session after the session has occurred.

Case Study

Introduction

This case example involves a required external evaluation for a five-year multicomponent educational reform project. The project was at the beginning of its second year, having contracted with a new evaluator to replace the first evaluator who had left the project for personal family reasons. In Year 1, an evaluation team had been identified but had last met eight months prior to review the original logic model and evaluation plan. The new evaluator began using working sessions with evaluation stakeholders a few years prior. She recognized this might be a useful strategy for reengaging the team in order to establish shared language and perspectives on the various components of the project and to focus the project's research and evaluation activity. She also reasoned that starting the session with the original logic model would provide an efficient means for updating her on the status of the project. Her key contact for the evaluation and member of the original evaluation team agreed. A member of the evaluation team, who had expressed enthusiasm about its value for helping guide the project during implementation, was also invited to work with the evaluator and the key contact to plan the meeting. This person had previously worked with most other team members; whereas the key contact had less overall experience

NEW DIRECTIONS FOR EVALUATION • DOI: 10.1002/ev

with the project and its staff. Together, the three women planned the working session.

Finding common meeting times had been difficult for the team in the past. The planners settled on a four-hour meeting with a working lunch, recognizing that setting the length of the meeting before fully detailing its specific objectives was necessary to get it on participants' calendars. They invited two new managers to join the team. One readily accepted; the other was hesitant due to his heavy workload—he had also been skeptical about the value of the evaluation. He remained reluctant but did agree to attend this first meeting because the evaluator asked him to provide input on project updates for revising the logic model. The email invitation to the meeting explained that its overall purpose was to reengage the evaluation team by establishing a common understanding of the project components and prioritizing the evaluation focus areas.

The planning group refined the overall purpose to name the three specific objectives shown in Exhibit 4.1. As the next step in the session, the evaluator proposed drafting a new evaluation plan for presentation, discussion, and revision at the next scheduled session. She described going from small-group input on revisions to different project areas and then large-group consensus on the overall logic model. From this work, the group could identify evaluation questions, and then give input on data collection methods. Thus, rather than the evaluator first providing direct technical assistance on the reliability, validity, and feasibility of different data collection methods, this approach would not only reveal different stakeholders' perspectives on methodology but also increase their ownership of the evaluation processes.

The Working Session

All but two persons invited attended. To the planners' disappointment, one was the program manager discussed earlier. Beginning with the third agenda item (C) in Exhibit 4.1, the following paragraphs describe the planned activities for the working session, their facilitation, and how each actually occurred.

Review of original logic model (20 min). Although the project's existing logic model had been sent out to participants for their individual review prior to the session, the planners realized that not everyone would have necessarily done so. A brief review of the logic model to give everyone a common starting point provided an opportunity to be reminded of its components and how they related to each other; this activity formed the basis for engaging small groups in revisions.

Small groups: Logic model revisions by project area (35 min). On the afternoon prior to the session, the planning group worked out preassignments for the small groups, placing four persons in each of three groups.

Two of the groups consisted of individuals who worked together on two different aspects of the project; the third group was a catch-all for the remaining stakeholders. The instructions to the group were:

1. Review the logic model, identify your areas of work, and discuss the accuracy of those areas as currently shown.
2. Name areas where components and linkages should be revised, being sure that each person proposing a revision gives a rationale.
3. Agree upon revisions for presentation to the larger group.
4. Make a list of any questions about any areas of the logic model that your group would like addressed in the whole group.

The planning team knew that the small groups might end up working on some of the same aspects of the logic model but reasoned that any differences in results among the groups would be important to discuss and resolve in the large group. One planning team member joined each of the small groups, with the evaluator choosing to go with the most heterogeneous group. Their role was to contribute to the discussion about logic model revisions where appropriate, and to help guide the small-group processes as necessary; but not to do the reporting out.

Large group: Small-group reporting and integration of results (80 min). The small-group reporting occurred as planned, with each of the groups describing their revisions. The three planners took different roles, with the evaluator facilitating the report-outs, one of the planners tracking the changes discussed on a projected image of the original logic model, and the other planner compiling the, as yet unresolved, questions from the small groups. The planners had expected there to be less difference among perspectives on many of the same areas of the logic model, particularly as the small groups described their rationales. This revealed that different staff members agreed about some details of implementing the project's main activities but gave widely varying perspectives on how a given activity was meant to contribute to short- and longer-term outcomes. Although discussing the implications of these differences (for both implementing and evaluating the project) was consuming additional agenda time, the evaluator knew it would be worth it. The group could reach perhaps a new and more deeply nuanced and shared understanding of how project activities were intended to result in various levels of expected outcomes. The group discussed the time issue and agreed to pursue the dialog. Ultimately, they decided that the input of the two absentees was needed to resolve two important questions.

During the large-group discussion, participants also surfaced concerns about contextual influences on the various components of the logic model. These emerged out of concern for how accurately the logic model depicted the project—especially as it was meant to provide a framework for the implementation evaluation. The strength and direction of various contextual influences were drawn in with arrows.

Development of evaluation questions for each logic model component and beyond (25 min). The previous dialog flowed easily into identifying evaluation questions for each component of the logic model, including the newly added contextual influences. The evaluator asked: "What would tell you if this activity is being (or was) successful?" Here some of the assumptions just surfaced, about how and why an activity would help achieve a desired outcome, came into play. With this information in mind, participants voiced new perspectives on the evaluation and what it should address.

Working lunch and prioritization of evaluation questions (30 min). The evaluator then asked participants to individually prioritize the 10 evaluation questions the group had just identified. Participants were asked to record their rankings next to the flip-charted evaluation questions. As the group enjoyed lunch, this relaxed activity was a break from the morning's more intense but cordial dialog. After about 20 minutes, one of the planners compiled the results, which revealed that seven of the evaluation questions were deemed approximately equally important. A second vote was taken among these seven questions, showing four of the questions to be of higher priority than the other three. The evaluator explained that the results from both of these votes would be helpful in making decisions about where to best expend evaluation resources.

Data collection methods for priority evaluation questions (10 min). With time running out, the evaluator proposed that they discuss data collection methods for only the top four evaluation questions. She asked the group, "What kinds of information would help you answer each of these four evaluation questions?" At first participants named the kinds of methods that had been included in the original evaluation plan. One participant, however, reminded the group of their earlier discussion on how and why certain activities were meant to lead to the desired outcomes. From here, several members of the group suggested that interviews with program participants would better reveal whether or not this had occurred than would the standardized survey instrument in the existing evaluation plan.

Review of next steps (7 min). At this point the evaluator had just enough time to scribble out and review the following next steps, the majority of which were to be her responsibility, but based upon the morning's results: (a) revise logic model and follow up with absentees, (b) draft evaluation plan based on the revised logic model, and (c) email the revised logic model and draft evaluation plan to the team to review before the next meeting. The group decided it would be more efficient to find a common meeting time for the next session when they were all together, and they did so.

Session debrief and closing (2 min). The session debrief had to be omitted, because time had run out. The evaluator had planned on asking each person to name a benefit they experienced from the session and something they would like to see happen at a future session. She quickly and clearly explained this to the group and asked if they would be willing to respond via email, and they agreed. About four individuals stayed after to make favorable comments about the session. One person appreciated getting to hear others' thinking the reasoning behind why particular project activities were meant to achieve outcomes. Another person agreed, adding that the project had never really explored some of these issues and they would now be approaching some things about implementing activities differently than before the session.

Planners' Debrief of the Session

The planners met later that afternoon to debrief. In the meantime, the evaluator sent out the email asking for feedback on the session, hoping to catch fresh thoughts from at least some of the participants. In about 90 minutes, they discussed their impressions of the session. Overall the three felt gratified that the session uncovered perspectives and assumptions within the group that may not otherwise have come forth, and that the ensuing dialog informed actionable items for both the project implementation and the evaluation. Because of this, they anticipated that the project would have a better chance of being truly successful and that the evaluation would be more relevant and accurate.

The evaluator volunteered to follow up with the two absentees. She hoped that (a) sharing and getting their input on the outcomes of the session would help engage them to some degree, as others had been at the meeting, and (b) each person would then be more likely to prioritize, as much as possible, their participation for future meetings.

The planners then focused on critiquing their facilitation skills. One person reflected that in his small group he felt he had been too directive at times, talking too much himself, and that he focused too much on his ideas about implementation based on updates to the project activities. Coincidentally, the evaluator also thought that too much of her own perspective about the project might have been coming into play in some of the large-group facilitation. Thinking about this issue for herself, the third planner wondered how this could be avoided; but on the other hand, she mentioned that she thought it was human nature. Sticking with the topic, the evaluator mentioned that she felt they could do more to explore their own values and assumptions. She knew about a series of questions they could ask themselves that would help surface their individual perspectives ahead of time, and in so doing reduce the "almost unconscious" need to get them voiced during the session. Her colleagues were intrigued and eager to begin their next planning session with the questions (see first row of Table 4.1).

Summary and Conclusions

In this case, the planning team for the working session used a variety of strategies and direct facilitation skills to bring about highly useful, if not unanticipated, results for refining implementation processes as well as developing a relevant evaluation plan with shared ownership. The strategies used included:

- Committing to the length of the session prior to establishing its specific objectives because of the urgency of getting the longer-than-normal meeting time onto participants' calendars.
- Including among the planners someone with long-standing working relationships with many of the participants.
- Waiting to provide technical assistance on evaluation methods until after getting initial participant input on data collection methods.
- Critiquing and taking action to improve facilitation skills.
- Following up directly with absentees soon after the session, specifically intending to engage them in the evaluation work and stimulate their interest in future participation.

The facilitation skills included:

- Varying the session's activities to maximize learning and engagement.
- Involving participants in procedural decisions during the session.
- Asking participants to explain their thinking.
- Knowing when an unanticipated dialog is worth having.
- Adjusting the agenda during the session and reconfiguring how to accomplish any agenda items not covered.

And finally, the specific facilitated activities used in the session were:

- A brief review of the logic model to give everyone a common starting point.
- Small-group input on revisions to different project areas and then large-group consensus on the overall logic model.
- Prioritization of evaluation questions.
- Discussion to establish appropriate data collection methods.
- Review of next steps and abbreviated closing.

With a heavy focus on process, the case addressed a number of issues, challenges, and successes in planning and facilitating evaluation working sessions. It is meant to show that:

- Working sessions can be undertaken without having been planned at the outset of the evaluation.
- The more planning that occurs, the greater likelihood of success.
- Being comfortable with the interplay between process and content and being willing to abandon a planned agenda can yield unanticipated results as good as, if not better than, those originally expected.

NEW DIRECTIONS FOR EVALUATION • DOI: 10.1002/ev

- Facilitation encompasses not only face-to-face interactions in a group setting, but also the specific strategies designed to make those interactions productive in a particular way: The constructivist and shared learning that occurs when heretofore unsurfaced insights, perspectives, and potential actions emerge within a group of individuals.

References

De Coninck, J., Chaturvedi, K., Haagsma, B., Griffioen, H., & van der Glas, M. (2008). *Planning, monitoring and evaluation in development organizations: Sharing training and facilitation experiences.* Thousand Oaks, CA: Sage.

Patton, M. Q. (2012). *Essentials of utilization-focused evaluation.* Thousand Oaks, CA: Sage.

Preskill, H. S., & Torres, R. T. (1998). *Evaluative inquiry for learning in organizations.* Thousand Oaks, CA: Sage.

Torres, R. T. (2006). Continuous learning. In K. M. Hannum, J. W. Martineau, & C. Reinelt (Eds.), *Handbook of leadership development evaluation* (pp. 536–558). San Francisco, CA: Jossey-Bass.

Torres, R. T., & Preskill, H. (2001). Evaluation and organizational learning: Past, present, and future. *American Journal of Evaluation, 22,* 387–396.

Torres, R. T., Preskill, H. S., & Piontek, M. E. (2005). *Evaluation strategies for communicating and reporting: Enhancing learning in organizations* (2nd ed.). Thousand Oaks, CA: Sage.

Torres, R. T., Stone, S. P., Butkus, D., Hook, B., Casey, J., Arens, S. A. (2000). Dialogue and reflection in a collaborative evaluation: Stakeholder and evaluator voices. In K. Ryan & L. Destefano (Eds.), *Evaluation as a democratic process: Promoting inclusion, dialogue, and deliberation. New Directions for Evaluation, 85,* 27–38.

ROSALIE T. TORRES *is principal of Torres Consulting Group, a New Orleans–based evaluation and management consulting firm specializing in the feedback-based development of programs and organizations, with a 35-year evaluation career that has included university teaching, professional development, and publications articulating practice-based theories of evaluation use; the relationship between evaluation and individual, team, and organizational learning; and evaluation communication strategies.*

NEW DIRECTIONS FOR EVALUATION • DOI: 10.1002/ev

Stevahn, L., & King, J. A. (2016). Facilitating interactive evaluation practice: Engaging stakeholders constructively. In R. S. Fierro, A. Schwartz, & D. H. Smart (Eds.), *Evaluation and
Facilitation. New Directions for Evaluation, 149*, 67–80.

5

Facilitating Interactive Evaluation Practice: Engaging Stakeholders Constructively

Laurie Stevahn, Jean A. King

Abstract

*This chapter introduces interactive evaluation practice (IEP) and its potential
for grounding thinking about the foundational nature of interaction in evaluation studies and the role of facilitation in this process. It begins by defining key terms and elaborating specifically on IEP as an evaluator orientation
for grounding and guiding decisions, actions, and reflections—all leveraged toward conducting meaningful studies. It then presents an evaluator's dozen of
strategies useful for facilitating interaction among stakeholders to accomplish
targeted aims and concludes by illustrating how evaluators can successfully
facilitate these strategies in practice.* © 2016 Wiley Periodicals, Inc., and the
American Evaluation Association.

valuation. Interaction. Facilitation. These three practices are often in-
separable when conducting program evaluation studies. The purpose of this chapter is to introduce interactive evaluation practice
(IEP) and its potential for grounding thinking about the foundational nature of interaction in framing, implementing, and reporting evaluation
studies—regardless of approach—and the role of facilitation in this process. We begin by defining key terms, then elaborate specifically on IEP
as an evaluator orientation for grounding and guiding decisions, actions,
and reflections—all leveraged toward conducting meaningful studies. We

continue by presenting an "evaluator's dozen" of strategies useful for facilitating interaction among various stakeholders to accomplish targeted aims that include (a) engaging people for interactive purposes (promoting positive relations, developing shared understandings, prioritizing/finalizing decisions, assessing evaluation progress), (b) carrying out basic inquiry tasks (framing evaluation questions, designing studies, sampling, collecting/ analyzing/interpreting/reporting results), and (c) involving people across increased levels of participation (responding/reacting to set information, generating content/input, organizing/synthesizing information for coherence). Finally, we illustrate how evaluators can facilitate these strategies in practice by providing practical examples centered on formulating a program's logic model, then validating it by collecting qualitative data from large samples when operating on a shoestring budget.

Definitions

We define *program evaluation* as "a process of systematic inquiry to provide sound information about the characteristics, activities, or outcomes of a program or policy for a valued purpose" (King & Stevahn, 2013, p. 13). This process places facilitation at the heart of what evaluators do—namely, interacting with stakeholders before, during, and after an evaluation toward framing, conducting, and reporting the study to address its valued purpose. Evaluators typically lead the way, given their central role in facilitating this process and the tasks it requires. In fact, our conceptualization of *interactive evaluation practice* (IEP) emerged from this realization. We argue that the evaluator's ability to interact with and involve stakeholders constructively at various points along the way is imperative to successful evaluation practice—regardless of approach, model, or methodology. Consequently, facilitating interaction with and among appropriate stakeholders throughout an evaluation toward providing sound results useful for intended purposes lies at the heart of what evaluators do.

Interactive evaluation practice is "the intentional act of engaging people in making decisions, taking action, and reflecting while conducting an evaluation study" (King & Stevahn, 2013, p. 14). Two key ideas ground IEP. First is the *personal factor* (Patton, 2008, 2012); this matters for evaluation use, because engaging key stakeholders increases the likelihood that evaluation findings will get used. Second is the *interpersonal factor* (King & Stevahn, 2013); this matters for actually conducting the evaluation, because creating, managing, and mastering interpersonal dynamics increase the likelihood of successfully interacting with and constructively involving others in doing the work of evaluation. Simply put, evaluators must interact with people, particularly primary intended users, to successfully conduct evaluations that will produce useful results and, therefore, must be able to skillfully facilitate interactions that promote constructive interpersonal dynamics with and among those involved.

NEW DIRECTIONS FOR EVALUATION • DOI: 10.1002/ev

Facilitation, defined in most dictionaries, is "the act of making easy or easier" (American Heritage Dictionary, 2000, p. 633). We doubt that many evaluators would refer to the practice of evaluation as easy; however, skilled evaluators often will take the lead in attempting to pave smooth pathways for interaction with and among stakeholders. Evaluators, for example, typically need to interact with a range of stakeholders, often starting with those who initiate and/or authorize studies—for example, conversations with the chief executive officer who sanctions the study, the division leader who prepares the request for qualifications and supervises external hiring, the department head who assigns internal personnel to manage the study, the funder who provides essential resources, and so on. In a similar fashion, evaluators also must be able to engage with those whose participation becomes central to accomplishing the study's purpose, such as involving organizational members for capacity building or seeking input and data from clients served by the organization. We therefore define facilitation as the plans and actions evaluators make and take to engage with stakeholders directly, as well as to engage stakeholders with each other, in ways that support constructive evaluation processes likely to produce useful results.

Distinguishing IEP and Its Facilitation Imperative

Basically, IEP is a way of thinking about evaluation practice that overtly recognizes the central role that interaction plays in successfully conducting evaluation studies. It therefore is not an evaluation approach or model governed by a set of rules applied in a mechanical step-by-step fashion, nor is it the application of facilitation principles to use in evaluation studies. Instead, IEP is an orientation to evaluation that concretely names the central role of interaction in conducting nearly all evaluation studies—much like calling attention to a need that frequently goes unnamed, such as oxygen for humans, water for fish, or soil for plants. Whether a study is more evaluator-directed, collaborative, or participant-directed, all evaluations require evaluators to interact and/or facilitate interaction at some level with and among people. Engaging appropriate others, enabling positive participation with and among those needed for a study to be developed, contracted, conducted, reported, and ultimately used—these interactions and their outcomes fundamentally affect and shape evaluations and their ability to meaningfully address concerns.

IEP's intentional focus on interpersonal interaction deliberately shifts evaluator attention to facilitation that promotes constructive dynamics among those involved. This means that technical competencies—such as clarifying and framing evaluation purposes and questions; determining appropriate designs, approaches, or models; sampling, collecting, and analyzing data; and interpreting and reporting results—must share center stage with the interpersonal competencies that enable such tasks to be planned, agreed upon, and carried out. In fact, recently developed evaluator competency frameworks around the world all emphasize interpersonal and facilitation skills, as summarized in Table 5.1.

An Evaluator's Dozen of Interactive Strategies

Bringing an IEP lens to facilitation means recognizing the value of developing a repertoire (toolbox) of basic strategies useful for constructively engaging stakeholders in evaluation. Over the years, we have come to rely on what we call an "evaluator's dozen" (i.e., 13) of interactive strategies because of their potential for establishing positive interdependence among participants, thereby making cooperative and collaborative efforts more likely (see *social interdependence theory* in Deutsch, 2006; Johnson & Johnson, 2013; King & Stevahn, 2013). Although many strategies beyond those presented in Table 5.2 may fruitfully facilitate various dimensions of evaluation practice (e.g., see Preskill & Russ-Eft, 2005; Stevahn & King, 2010), we tend to draw repeatedly upon these 13 because of their broad and effective applicability across diverse evaluation contexts, settings, approaches, models, methodologies, and purposes.

Selecting Strategies for Facilitation

How do evaluators decide which strategies to facilitate in any given situation? Skilled facilitators know there is no easy answer. Much depends on the overall goals of the evaluation and specific objectives of any facilitation, in addition to understanding the situational context, particular circumstances, and unique qualities of participants—carefully watching throughout to determine how best to attend to observed needs. In fact, developing a "sixth sense" becomes important for making judicious choices, paying special attention to interpersonal nuance and social cues (Stevahn & King, 2014). There are, however, three key facilitation considerations that, in general, guide decision making: What *outcomes* are desired? How much *time* is available? What level of *involvement* does each strategy require?

Outcomes. When deciding which of the evaluator's dozen strategies to facilitate, first consider what each will produce. *Strategies 1–4* promote positive interpersonal relations among participating stakeholders, as when those serving on a newly formed steering committee come together to frame and manage the evaluation throughout its duration. *Strategies 2–10* result in shared understandings, as when participants grapple with identifying and deciding how best to allocate resources to accomplish evaluation tasks. *Strategies 11–13* enable prioritizing and finalizing decisions, as when stakeholders deliberate which recommendations to enact immediately. Finally, all of the strategies can be used to involve stakeholders in assessing evaluation progress and determining how best to adjust procedures when warranted.

Time. Next, consider time available for facilitation. *Strategies 1–6, 9, 12,* and *13* typically can be facilitated relatively quickly (5–20 minutes),

NEW DIRECTIONS FOR EVALUATION • DOI: 10.1002/ev

Table 5.1. Evaluator Competency Frameworks and Interpersonal Facilitation Skills (ordered by year; original numbers/bullets/formats maintained)

Evaluator Competency Framework	*Interpersonal Domains and Competencies*
Essential Competencies for Program Evaluators (Stevahn, King, Ghere, & Minnema, 2005)	6.0 Interpersonal Competence 6.5 Facilitates constructive interpersonal interaction (teamwork, group facilitation, processing)
Evaluator Competencies (International Board of Standards for Training, Performance and Instruction, 2006; Russ-Eft, Bober, de la Teja, Foxon, & Koszalka, 2008)	Professional Foundations 3. Demonstrate effective interpersonal skills

Competencies for Canadian Evaluation Practice (Canadian Evaluation Society, 2010)	5.0 Interpersonal Practice
	   5.6 Uses facilitation skills (group work)
	   5.7 Uses interpersonal skills (individual and teams)

Aotearoa New Zealand Evaluation Association Evaluator Competencies (Aotearoa New Zealand Evaluation Association, 2011)	Evaluation management and professional evaluation practice • A demonstrated ability to develop collaborative, cooperative, and respective relationships with those involved in and affected by the evaluation (stakeholders) and evaluation team members by: • Building relationships and developing engagement and commitment
The EES Evaluation Capabilities Framework (European Evaluation Society, 2011)	2. Professional practice 2.2 Displays interpersonal skills
Competencies for Development Evaluation Evaluators, Managers, and Commissioners (International Development Evaluation Association, 2012)	7.0 Promoting a Culture of Learning from Evaluation 7.3 Champions evaluation and seeks to build the evaluation capacity of others
Evaluators' Professional Learning Competency Framework (Australasian Evaluation Society, 2013)	6. Interpersonal Skills • Have the capacity to build relationships with a range of people • Use facilitation skills (group work), interpersonal skills (individual and teams), and conflict resolution skills to elicit robust qualitative input to evaluation data

NEW DIRECTIONS FOR EVALUATION • DOI: 10.1002/ev

Table 5.2. Interactive Strategies for Facilitating Stakeholder Involvement in Evaluation Practice (further detailed in King & Stevahn, 2013)

Interactive Strategy	Facilitation Purpose and Outcome
1. Voicing Variables	To learn about similarities and differences across participants, such as personal characteristics, experiences, perspectives, desires. Produces visual frequency counts of participants regarding relevant options/variables
2. Voicing Viewpoints/Beliefs	To forge and/or refine shared understandings, perceptions, or beliefs about various aspects of evaluation. Produces explicit Likert-scale responses that reveal individual value orientations useful for exploring interpretations and grounding conversations toward developing collective understandings
3. Choosing Corners	To reveal diverse perspectives, discuss underlying rationales, and foster deeper understanding on a topic or issue. Produces visual frequency counts of participants' perspectives according to four response options for each issue
4. Cooperative Interviews	To discover similar characteristics among participants who rotate the roles of interviewer, responder, and recorder within a small group of three. Produces written self-disclosure from which overall commonalities/themes emerge within and across small groups
5. Round-Robin/ Check-In	To gather input from all participants systematically (sequentially) and quickly (sound-bite responses) on a topic. Produces information that reveals what is most meaningful (formative assessment), reinforces key ideas (shared impact), or illuminates constructive next steps (future direction)
6. Making Metaphors/Sharing Similes	To reveal new insights by identifying patterns, similar qualities, and/or unique outliers based on participants' responses to a question or topic. Produces metaphors expressed in words/phrases or visual images, such as photos, pictures, postcards, or objects
7. Data Dialogue	To obtain divergent input/opinions from people (often large numbers) organized in small groups (of three or four individuals). Produces written input (one volunteer scribe per group) on several questions useful for qualitative analysis across groups to produce overarching themes
8. Jigsaw	To understand an entire body of information by dividing it (like jigsaw puzzle pieces) among group members who each learn and teach their unique part to everyone in their group. Produces a better understood whole, useful for making decisions or determining next steps
9. Graffiti/Carousel	To obtain input (graffiti) from participants organized in teams to respond to diverse topics (each on separate chart papers that rotate across teams). Produces chart papers filled with notes/comments/input on each topic, ready for analysis, synthesis, and reporting

(Continued)

Table 5.2. Continued

Interactive Strategy	Facilitation Purpose and Outcome
10. Concept Formation/Cluster Maps	To summarize a set of data through qualitative content analysis. Produces labeled clusters of like items (major themes), that then may be visually mapped to show connections and relationships (similar to word webs or mind maps)
11. Cooperative Rank Order	To reach consensus on a rank, order, or sequence for a set of items (such as evaluation recommendations). Produces a linear list of items/steps in order of priority or preference
12. Fist-to-Five	To identify shared (or diverse) characteristics, ideas, orientations, or priorities by asking individuals to show a *fist,* or *one, two, three, four, five* fingers (similar to a semantic differential survey item) to a targeted topic provided by the facilitator. Produces visual public display of frequencies/percentages that indicate degree/strength of participant responses
13. Dot Votes/Bar Graphs	To collectively prioritize alternatives for future decision making. Produces charts/options with sticky dots or notes showing frequencies of what is desired, preferred, or valued for each option

whereas *Strategies 2* and *7–11* usually take longer (30–60 minutes or more). Here, tradeoffs are inevitable; a strategy may be perfect for accomplishing a particular outcome, but without enough time to properly facilitate, the risk of frustrating participants is great, defeating the purpose and derailing success. Ultimately, the time required for any given strategy may depend most on the complexity of the content, information, or material that participants will generate or examine (whether relatively simple or elaborately detailed), the gravity of the targeted outcome (whether final and binding or formative and advisory), and the skills that facilitators and participants bring to the task (whether fluent from prior experience or first-time users).

Involvement. Finally, consider the types of involvement that each strategy requires. *Strategies 1–3, 8,* and *10–13* primarily involve stakeholders in responding to existing content and information, as when providing feedback on a set of given evaluation questions or program recommendations. *Strategies 4–9* involve stakeholders in generating new content and information, as when responding to open-ended prompts that produce insights on what matters most for effective program delivery. *Strategies 8* and *10–13* involve stakeholders in organizing or preparing to share or present information regardless of its origin, as when deciding which results need immediate attention and how best to sequence these in the final report or presentation. These three broad types of involvement place different demands on participating stakeholders, requiring different levels of intensity—some more, others less. Collectively analyzing input to generate evaluation

Figure 5.1. Logic Model Template

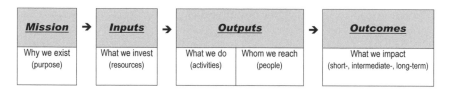

recommendations, for example, requires deeper cognitive investment and social engagement than reacting to an already formulated set.

An Example: Facilitating Strategies to Develop and Validate a Logic Model

As any facilitator knows, it is often straightforward to describe strategies, but another thing altogether to put them into practice in real situations. The scenario that follows illustrates how evaluators may facilitate the evaluator's dozen to engage stakeholders constructively in developing a program's logic model, then collect qualitative data from large representative samples toward validating the model—all on a shoestring budget. Although situated in education, consider how the scenario and facilitations may be applied in other contexts such as health, business, government, nonprofit, and other organizational settings—especially yours.

Imagine a university with approximately 5,000 students enrolled in undergraduate and graduate programs. Its mission focuses not only on teaching academic disciplines, but also on preparing professionals and leaders to work together for a just and humane world. This commitment to social justice permeates every aspect of the university, including decisions about instructional programs, required courses, learning outcomes, teaching methods, assigned materials, and student assessments. In preparation for an upcoming evaluation, the dean of one of the largest colleges on campus hired an external evaluator to assist in constructing a *logic model* to map *inputs* (resources), *outputs* (activities and processes and people and programs), and *outcomes* (short-term, intermediate, and long-term impact)—along with identifying underlying assumptions about how these intersect to accomplish *mission* (purpose for existing), which, at this university, focuses on preparing advocates for social justice in their respective professional fields of practice. The evaluator decided to use the logic model outlined in Figure 5.1 as a template throughout the process.

The dean and evaluator agreed that input from department chairs, program directors, faculty, staff, students, and graduates of the college would be important to developing the model, so a representative task force of 18 was established to convene twice—each a full-day session—once in the fall, then again in the spring. The first meeting began with a welcome from the dean who charged the task force with its work, explained anticipated benefits to the college and its stakeholders, reviewed the timeline for completion, and then introduced the evaluator who proceeded to facilitate the following strategies throughout the day.

- *Strategy 1: Voicing Variables.* After briefly sharing additional background information and restating the goal of the session (to prepare a logic model depicting how the college empowers leaders for a just and humane world), the evaluator asked participants to stand in response to several variables: (a) primary role (student, faculty, administrator, staff, graduate of the college), (b) number of years associated with the college (5 or less, 6–10, beyond 10), and (c) something especially appreciated about the university (its leadership, focus on excellence, cultural and ethnic diversity, ethos of caring, community connections, special programs/ events, other factors). This quickly provided interpersonal grounding and connection.
- *Strategy 2: Voicing Viewpoints/Beliefs.* The evaluator then provided everyone with a half-sheet containing the following statement: "Visibility is the key to effective leadership for social justice." Individuals circled their own Likert-scale response (*strongly agree, agree, disagree, strongly disagree*)— again, a quick way to direct attention and reflection on the underlying purpose of the logic model.
- *Strategy 3: Choosing Corners.* To further explore and clarify participants' beliefs about effective leadership for justice, the evaluator posted the four Likert-scale responses from the previous activity, each in a separate corner of the room, then invited everyone to (a) move to the corner matching one's own response, (b) connect with one or two others in the corner, and (c) discuss reasons for choosing that response. Hearing rationales reported out from each corner enabled everyone to better understand that overall people believed what mattered most about effective leadership centered on communicating and acting for social justice consistently across all situations, whether or not highly visible, but with a preference for visibility, transparency, and sustained focus.
- *Strategy 4: Cooperative Interviews.* To further nurture positive relations plus reveal qualities important to realizing social justice, the evaluator then arranged teams of three, each identifying an *interviewer, responder,* and *recorder*—rotating roles three times so that teammates eventually performed each role. The interview involved recalling a lived experience that increased personal commitment to social justice—what, where, when, why, how. Reviewing the notes depicting each story, teammates identified common qualities, then shared with the entire gathering, after which a master list of major themes emerged, including (a) direct experience, (b) deep reflection, (c) challenged assumptions, (d) honest conversation, (e) memorable media/materials/images, (f) opportunities and invitations

to act, and (g) real-life stories of those oppressed and those acting for justice. These would serve as touchstones later in the session.

- *Strategy 9: Graffiti/Carousel*. Now the focus turned toward using the prior background information to map the logic model. The evaluator established four teams (each comprised of four or five people) and provided each with one chart paper containing a different question related to developing leaders for social justice: (a) What do we invest (resources) in developing leaders for social justice? (b) What do we do (activities) to develop such leaders? (c) Whom do we reach (people—internal and external)? (d) What are the impacts (positive changes)? These four topics rotated clockwise every 60 seconds across all four teams. Individuals wrote ideas on each topic (as many as possible, one per sticky note), randomly placing all notes on the charts as they shifted from team to team. This rapidly generated lots of input, maximizing voice and involvement.

- *Strategy 10: Concept Formation/Cluster Maps*. Each team then took one of the four topics (i.e., resources, activities, people, or changes) and organized the "graffiti" (sticky notes) on its chart paper into content-alike clusters/groups/themes. This involved comparing and contrasting items, thinking critically, listening to teammates, and reaching agreement on final sorting, so it took a bit more time.

- *Strategy 13: Dot Votes/Bar Graphs*. Debriefing began by asking each team to share its themes. The first team reported themes related to *resources*. These included (a) support for faculty professional development, (b) an endowed visiting professor position for diversity and justice, (c) student scholarships for study abroad, (d) social media sites for justice-related announcements, (e) blogs for sharing insights and reflections, and so on. Each was written on a separate sheet of paper posted on the wall. Participants then received three sticky dots, and individuals quickly placed theirs on three different resources deemed most essential to developing leaders for social justice. The resources were then written on the logic model in order, from highest to lowest tallies.

- *Strategy 10: Concept Formation/Cluster Maps*. The second team reported themes related to *activities*. These included (a) integrating justice content/materials into all courses as appropriate, (b) requiring a signature core course on social justice in professional practice, (c) involving students in academic service-learning and/or community-based research projects, (d) providing opportunities for study abroad experiences to enhance global justice, (e) sponsoring faculty workshops to enhance teaching for social justice, (f) hosting special events on leadership for justice, and others. Together, the entire gathering reflected on these in light of the qualities and characteristics that emerged from the cooperative interview activity conducted earlier (many were related or aligned), then created a cluster/bubble map, with branches from each theme, specifying its "pluses" and "minuses." This analysis required time for discussion and agreement on the final order for listing the themes on the logic model—time well spent to forge shared understanding of those items deemed most feasible and advantageous for promoting student growth.

- *Strategy 12: Fist-to-Five.* The third team reported themes related to *people* associated with the activities. One by one, the evaluator read aloud: (a) university/college students, (b) faculty, (c) administrators, (d) policy makers, (e) project funders, (f) community organizations and programs that host student interns or hire graduates, and so on. While acknowledging that all matter, the participants responded to each by showing a *fist* through *five fingers*—denoting *low* to *high* importance for focus—and mean scores were estimated and recorded for each. This occurred quickly, resulting in a ranking from *most* to *less* important, sequenced this way on the logic model.
- *Strategy 11: Cooperative Rank Order.* The fourth team reported themes related to *change*—that is, expected positive outcomes/impacts. The participants formed pairs, wrote the themes on 3 × 5 cards (one per card), then sequenced the cards/themes from short-, to intermediate-, to long-term effects. The pairs taped their rankings to a large sheet of paper, then posted them on the wall. Looking across all postings, similar patterns emerged, resulting in discussion and agreement on how to order these anticipated effects on the logic model's *outcome/impact* continuum.
- *Strategy 6: Making Metaphors/Sharing Similes.* The session ended by asking participants to select a photograph from a collection cut from magazines to complete this sentence: "Our work today especially reminded me that empowering leadership for social justice will happen when. ..." Each person shared his/her photo and reason for choosing it, which again reinforced collective purpose and provided a sense of accomplishment.

Before the spring meeting, the evaluator collected qualitative input to validate the logic model from samples representing three populations—students, graduates, and faculty. This occurred at three already-scheduled college events—a student job fair, an alumni event, and a faculty meeting. The following strategy was used with those at each event.

- *Strategy 7: Data Dialogue.* After introductions, the evaluator arranged groups of three or four people, asking each to appoint a scribe. Groups then were given two sheets for recording diverse input from members on the following questions: (a) What does it mean to be a leader for social justice in your professional field of practice? (b) What university experiences or activities related to social justice most changed you, and in what ways?

At the spring task-force meeting, all faculty in the college joined the stakeholders who participated in the fall session to review the data dialogue results and consider alignment with the logic model. The evaluator facilitated the following strategies:

- *Strategy 5: Round-Robin/Check-In.* The session opened by asking each participant to respond with a "sound bite" to this question: "What fuels your commitment to social justice?" Participants shared words and phrases such as "income inequality," "experiencing injustice," "moral convictions," "the university mission," and "life, liberty, and the pursuit of happiness for all." This brief yet telling self-disclosure created a sense of connection and shared identity as individuals listened to each other's responses.
- *Strategy 8: Jigsaw.* Next, the evaluator arranged teams of three, giving each the analyzed data dialogue results from only one of the three samples—students, graduates, or faculty. Each team studied/learned its assigned material and decided how best to present it to others—then new teams of three were formed comprised of one person to share the student findings, one to share the graduate findings, and one to share the faculty findings. After the presentations, the teammates identified similarities and differences across the three sets of findings and then discussed overall alignment with the logic model. Each team shared its thinking with the entire gathering, which led to minor revisions of the logic model and greater understanding of its components, underlying assumptions, and expectations.

By the end of the spring session, the evaluator had successfully facilitated a process that both involved a sizeable number of stakeholders giving significant input and resulted in a logic model entirely built on that input. Throughout, the evaluator considered each strategy's purpose (products that would result), time available (versus time needed for strategy implementation), material/content to be addressed (simple or complex, familiar or new), and demands on participants (quick or brief responses/encounters versus sustained interaction for deeper understanding or mutual decision making). At each gathering, the evaluator constantly monitored reactions and interactions to appropriately pace activities, assess the effectiveness of facilitation choices, and make adjustments for success based on observed needs.

Conclusion

Although not all evaluators see their role as one of facilitator, we argue that interaction is inextricably part of evaluation practice, so paying attention to interpersonal dynamics and how to facilitate interaction is not only worth the effort, but necessary. We also argue that *cooperative* interactive strategies in particular—like many that comprise the evaluator's dozen—are especially useful because they promote an increased sense of commitment to working together to achieve common goals. Finally, it is through interaction that inclusion, voice, culture, context, situational responsiveness, and constructive conflict become lived realities in evaluation studies, increasing the potential for meaningful processes that produce useful results. Evaluators who skillfully facilitate such interaction play pivotal roles in paving pathways for success.

References

The American Heritage Dictionary of the English Language. (2000). *Facilitation*. Boston, MA: Houghton Mifflin.

Aotearoa New Zealand Evaluation Association. (2011). *Aotearoa New Zealand Evaluation Association evaluator competencies*. Retrieved from http://www.anzea.org.nz/wp-content/uploads/2013/05/110801_anzea_evaluator_competencies_final.pdf

Australasian Evaluation Society. (2013). *Evaluators' professional learning competency framework*. Retrieved from http://www.aes.asn.au/images/stories/files/Professional%20Learning/AES_Evaluators_Competency_Framework.pdf

Canadian Evaluation Society. (2013). *Competencies for Canadian evaluation practice*. Retrieved from http://www.evaluationcanada.ca/txt/2_competencies_cdn_evaluation_practice.pdf

Deutsch, M. (2006). Cooperation and competition. In M. Deutsch, P. T. Coleman, & E. C. Marcus (Eds.), *The handbook of conflict resolution: Theory and practice* (2nd ed., pp. 3–42). San Francisco, CA: Jossey-Bass.

European Evaluation Society. (2011). *The EES evaluation capabilities framework*. Retrieved from http://www.europeanevaluation.org/sites/default/files/surveys/EES%20EVALUATION%20CAPABILITIES%20FRAMEWORK.pdf

International Board of Standards for Training, Performance and Instruction. (2006). *Evaluator competencies*. Retrieved from http://ibstpi.org/evaluator-competencies/

International Development Evaluation Association. (2012). *Competencies for development evaluation evaluators, managers, and commissioners*. Retrieved from http://ideas-global.org/competencies-for-development-evaluators/

Johnson, D. W., & Johnson, F. P. (2013). *Joining together: Group theory and group skills* (11th ed.). Boston, MA: Pearson Education.

King, J. A., & Stevahn, L. (2013). *Interactive evaluation practice: Mastering the interpersonal dynamics of program evaluation*. Thousand Oaks, CA: Sage.

Patton, M. Q. (2008). *Utilization focused evaluation* (4th ed.). Thousand Oaks, CA: Sage.

Patton, M. Q. (2012). *Essentials of utilization-focused evaluation*. Thousand Oaks, CA: Sage.

Preskill, H., & Russ-Eft, D. (2005). *Building evaluation capacity: 72 activities for teaching and training*. Thousand Oaks, CA: Sage.

Russ-Eft, D., Bober, M. J., de la Teja, I., Foxon, M. J., & Koszalka, T. A. (2008). *Evaluator competencies: Standards for the practice of evaluation in organizations*. San Francisco, CA: Jossey-Bass.

Stevahn, L., & King, J. A. (2010). *Needs assessment: Phase III taking action for change*. Thousand Oaks, CA: Sage.

Stevahn, L., & King, J. A. (2014). What does it take to be an effective qualitative evaluator? Essential competencies. In L. Goodyear, J. Jewiss, J. Usinger, & E. Barela (Eds.), *Qualitative inquiry in evaluation: From theory to practice* (pp. 141–166). San Francisco, CA: Jossey-Bass.

Stevahn, L., King, J. A., Ghere, G., & Minnema, J. (2005). Establishing essential competencies for program evaluators. *American Journal of Evaluation, 26*, 43–59.

LAURIE STEVAHN *is a professor in the Educational Leadership Doctoral Program in the College of Education at Seattle University.*

JEAN A. KING *is a professor in the Department of Organizational Leadership, Policy, and Development and director of the Minnesota Evaluation Studies Institute (MESI) at the University of Minnesota.*

NEW DIRECTIONS FOR EVALUATION • DOI: 10.1002/ev

Pankaj, V., & Emery, A. K. (2016). Data placemats: A facilitative technique designed to enhance stakeholder understanding of data. In R. S. Fierro, A. Schwartz, & D. H. Smart (Eds.), *Evaluation and Facilitation. New Directions for Evaluation, 149,* 81–93.

6

Data Placemats: A Facilitative Technique Designed to Enhance Stakeholder Understanding of Data

Veena Pankaj, Ann K. Emery

Abstract

This chapter introduces data placemats, a facilitative technique that occurs during the analysis stage of an evaluation that is designed to enhance stakeholder understanding of evaluation data. Data placemats display thematically grouped data designed to encourage stakeholder interaction with collected data and to promote the cocreation of meaning under the facilitative guidance of the evaluator. Each placemat represents the data using visual elements such as charts, graphs, and quotes and draws on best practices of data and information display to format these elements. During the process, evaluators guide stakeholders to a mutual understanding of information contained in the data placemats. This chapter provides guidance on when, why, and how to use data placemats to enhance the overall sense-making of data and explores the connection between effective facilitation and successful implementation of this technique. © 2016 Wiley Periodicals, Inc., and the American Evaluation Association.

Decades of research on participatory evaluation have paved the way for understanding the connections between stakeholder involvement, stakeholder buy-in, and the overall utility of evaluation findings for action and improvement (Cousins & Chouinard, 2012). From the work of our predecessors, we understand the value of engaging stakeholders in all phases of the evaluation life cycle. A number of facilitation techniques can be used to involve stakeholders in the planning phase of evaluation, such as the collaborative development of logic models through visual mapping exercises, group brainstorming to develop evaluation questions, and various voting techniques to prioritize the focus of the evaluation. Opportunities for stakeholder participation in the later stages—especially during analysis—are often overlooked.

In this chapter, we discuss a facilitative process designed to enhance stakeholder buy-in and understanding of data that can be employed during the analysis phase of the evaluation lifecycle. When used correctly, this process can help facilitate the analysis of data in a collaborative setting. Figure 6.1 illustrates the key components of this process. First, the evaluator analyzes data and organizes preliminary findings in the form of *data placemats*. Next, the evaluator facilitates a *data interpretation meeting* during which the evaluator guides stakeholders through the process of reading charts and verbalizing the key findings in their own words. Finally, the evaluator conducts *additional analyses* and produces a *final report* or other deliverable.

Figure 6.1. The Facilitative Process at a Glance

Phase 1	Phase 2	Phase 3
Evaluator analyzes data and organizes preliminary findings in the form of **data placemats**	Evaluator facilitates a **data interpretation meeting** in which stakeholders verbalize the story being told in their own words	Evaluator conducts **additional analysis** (if needed) and produces a **final deliverable**, such as a report or presentation

This facilitative process requires that the evaluator employs a combination of tools and techniques, including data placemats, data interpretation meetings, and facilitation skills.

Data Placemats

A *data placemat* is an 11-by-17-inch sheet of paper that displays thematically grouped data in the form of charts, graphs, and quotes. Depending on the magnitude of the evaluation and the number of evaluation questions to be answered, evaluators may design anywhere between three and twelve different placemats. Data placemats allow the evaluator to share preliminary evaluation findings with stakeholders before presenting final evaluation findings. Sample data placemats are shown in Figure 6.2.

NEW DIRECTIONS FOR EVALUATION • DOI: 10.1002/ev

Figure 6.2. General Design of Data Placemats

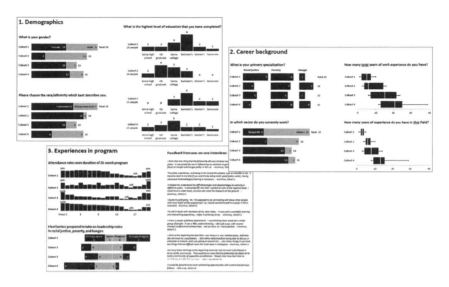

Data Interpretation Meetings

A *data interpretation meeting* is usually a two- to three-hour facilitated session in which the evaluator presents the data placemats and guides stakeholders through a process of interpreting and drawing meaning from data. During the evaluation life cycle, evaluators often gather information from multiple perspectives to help answer key evaluation questions. However, it is less common to provide an opportunity for stakeholders to weigh in during the analysis process. It is at this juncture of the evaluation life cycle where stakeholder perspectives can offer the most insight. This meeting environment also allows stakeholders to cocreate new knowledge with each other and with the evaluator, a collaborative process not unlike the graphic recording process described by Dean-Coffey (2013).

Depending on the nature and duration of the evaluation, data interpretation meetings should be held after each significant data collection event. In a one-year evaluation, it may make sense to share data only at the end of all data collection activities; however, in a multiyear evaluation, we recommended sharing data at more frequent intervals. This is especially true for advocacy evaluations, where stakeholders need real-time information to make course corrections (Coffman & Reed, 2009).

Facilitation Skills: Facilitating Meetings and Facilitating a Learning Journey

Facilitation within this context relies on the evaluator's technical and adaptive abilities to navigate stakeholders between the three phases of

Table 6.1. Technical and Adaptive Capacities

Technical Capacities	Adaptive Capacities
• Data analysis • Preparing meeting materials (placemats, agenda, questions for discussions, etc.) • Designing placemats • Scheduling the meeting • Making sure the right people are in the room	• Perceiving and interpreting real-time events • Making in-the-moment course corrections • Flexibility • Ability to nurture the flow of productive conversation • Ability to rely on intuition and instinct

the learning journey and during the data interpretation meeting itself (see Table 6.1). Phase 1 of the learning journey—analyzing data and designing data placemats—draws heavily on the evaluator's technical capacities. Phase 2—facilitating a data interpretation meeting—draws heavily on the evaluator's adaptive capacities.

The following is an example of using some adaptive capacities while facilitating a data interpretation meeting.

One of our foundation clients wanted us to share evaluation findings with a variety of stakeholders, including foundation staff as well as a number of representatives from grantee organizations. Since this client was located in a different state, we decided to conserve evaluation resources by holding a single data interpretation meeting with all the different groups of stakeholders.

During the meeting with the foundation staff and grantees, we could tell from body language that the grantee stakeholders had not bought into the data or the process we were using to share the preliminary findings. The conversation felt stifled and was not adequately capturing the variety of viewpoints within the room. Using adaptive facilitation skills of perceiving and interpreting real-time events and incorporating flexibility, we realized that we needed to regroup and make mid-course corrections to our meeting agenda. At that moment, we paused the conversation surrounding the evaluation results and described what we felt was occurring within the room. The moment we acknowledged the grantees' discomfort and tension, we sensed that we had gained their respect. We learned that grantee organizations did not feel that their viewpoints were included in the initial evaluation planning stages.

Next, we gave participants a 10-minute break so that we could strategize about how to best rearrange the agenda. When we reconvened as a group, we asked the grantee organizations to describe the types of questions that they thought were useful to answer through the evaluation. We showed them the data placemats that contained information about those evaluation questions, and the rest of the conversation went smoothly.

NEW DIRECTIONS FOR EVALUATION • DOI: 10.1002/ev

Facilitating a Learning Journey

Data placemats and data interpretation meetings are intended to facilitate a learning journey among participating stakeholders. While most of this learning occurs during the data interpretation meeting, a considerable amount of evaluator preparation and facilitation must also take place before and after the data interpretation meeting.

Phase 1. Before the data interpretation meeting.   Preparing for a data interpretation meeting is critical for success. Before the meeting, the evaluator must collect and analyze data, visualize the data and design data placemats, and schedule the data interpretation meeting with the appropriate group of stakeholders. The evaluator is balancing familiar roles: that of data collector, data analyst, data visualizer, client liaison, and meeting planner.

Step 1.1. Conduct preliminary data analysis. First, the evaluator conducts a preliminary analysis of the quantitative and/or qualitative data that has been collected through the evaluation. A preliminary analysis of qualitative data might consist of gathering key quotes and noting high-level themes. A preliminary analysis of quantitative data might involve descriptive statistics, frequencies, and simple cross-tabulations.

The goal is to involve stakeholders in the analysis process before results are complete and to use stakeholders' ideas as inspiration for areas in which to calculate inferential statistics to be included in the final report. The example below describes using stakeholders' reflections about preliminary analysis to inform future analysis.

During a 10-year retrospective evaluation of a one-year fellowship program, the fellowship program's management team was interested in program satisfaction rates. In particular, the management team sought to understand how fellows felt about the training curriculum, and the structure of the fellowship, their cohort of fellows, and the overall fellowship experience. When designing the data placemats, we included graphs that displayed satisfaction survey data about each of these topics.

During our data interpretation meeting, the funders noticed there was a substantial dip in satisfaction rates in Year 4 of the fellowship program. Using adaptive facilitation techniques, we were able to create a space for the management team to openly discuss potential reasons for this decline. The management team reflected upon Year 4 and remembered that there had been a change in recruitment strategies, which affected the type and number of people who were recruited.

With that information in hand, after the data interpretation meeting, we were able to go back to our office and map out the specific changes that were made in the recruitment process and explore the connections between the

New Directions for Evaluation • DOI: 10.1002/ev

programmatic changes and satisfaction rates across multiple variables. The data interpretation meeting enabled us to take a deeper dive into the data to better understand patterns and trends in the data and offer concrete suggestions for future recruitment.

Step 1.2. Design the data placemat(s). When designing data placemats, the evaluator decides which preliminary patterns should be discussed during the data interpretation meeting; creates charts in Microsoft Excel or other data visualization software programs; and pastes the charts into Microsoft PowerPoint or Word.

During this stage, the evaluator is an *information architect*, a term coined by Richard Saul Wurman to describe the "professionals trained in organizing data and making sense of it" (as cited in Cairo, 2013, p. 15). As described by Cairo (2013), "Wurman suggests that one of the main goals of information architecture is to help users avoid information anxiety, the 'black hole between data and knowledge'" (p. 15). Similarly, when applied to an evaluative context, the evaluator is a *data architect*: The evaluator constructs a data placemat or blueprint that contains answers to the stakeholders' evaluation questions and then guides stakeholders down the path of interpretation during the data interpretation meeting.

On the surface, data placemats appear to be a simple collage of charts, but there are a number of intentional design decisions involved—described by Cairo (2013) as "not just an art" but as "the careful and restrained tinkering of an engineer" (p. 23).

- First, the evaluator chooses which pieces of data belong in the placemat based on his or her best guesses, assumptions, and instincts about the stakeholders' interests and information needs.
- Second, the evaluator chooses how to use color to draw attention—or not—to patterns in the data. Evergreen and Metzner (2013) state that "color is one of the quickest elements to capture attention" (p. 11) in data visualizations and they argue that "for color to be used well, secondary information or data points should be simplified to a shade of gray so that chosen elements can appropriately stand out when selected emphasis is applied" (p. 9). A key principle throughout this three-phase facilitation process is that the evaluator is creating a space for stakeholders to interpret data for themselves. Accordingly, data placemats should not draw stakeholders' attention to any single pattern over another. Figure 6.3 illustrates the distinction between using a monochromatic color scheme when designing a data placemat (left) and selectively drawing attention to one takeaway message when designing charts for a final report (right). The frequency counts are identical, the small multiples histograms are identical, but the shading is intentionally different.
- Third, the evaluator chooses how much and what type of text to include. Data placemats should include generic titles, subtitles, and labels,

Figure 6.3. Graphs With and Without Color Emphasis and Interpretive Text for Data Placemats (Left) and Final Reports (Right)

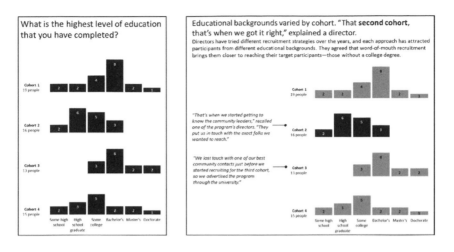

but should not include interpretive text—again, so that stakeholders can draw their own conclusions about which pieces of the story are most important in the data interpretation meeting. Figure 6.3 also illustrates the distinction between generic text for a data placemat (left) and interpretive text for a final report (right). Chart titles in data placemats should only indicate the corresponding survey question or data source. Once the evaluator listens to stakeholders' reflections during the data interpretation meeting, these stories and contextual details are added to the chart through titles, subtitles, and/or annotations and included in the final report.

We recommend grouping charts by evaluation question; that is, one placemat per evaluation question. Data interpretation meetings flow best with three to twelve total placemats. The final placemats are printed on 11-by-17-inch paper so that stakeholders have adequate space to sketch and take notes on the placemats.

Step 1.3. Determine who should attend. It is important to include people who are most involved with the program and have a stake in the evaluation. This includes line staff, supervisors, and may also include an involved board member. Based on the size of the program/initiative being evaluated, a data interpretation meeting could work well with as few as two or three participants and as many as six to eight participants. Additional factors to consider as you determine who to invite to the meeting include:

1) *Power dynamics.* Are there certain voices that carry more weight than others? Is there a dominant person in the room whose voice tends

to shape the conversation? Will the personality and position dynamics within the room yield to candid conversations? These considerations are described in the American Evaluation Association's Cultural
Competence Statement (Fairhaven, 2011) and Guiding Principles for
Evaluators (American Evaluation Association, 2004).

2) *Willingness to share.* Are the people in the room ready to "roll up their
   sleeves" and have an open and honest conversation about the data
   and its implications? Will people feel comfortable talking about things
   that may not be working well?

Depending on the size of the group or the potential dynamics of the
participants, it may be helpful to hold more than one data interpretation
meeting. It is up to the evaluator, with guidance from the client, to determine what mix of individuals will yield fruitful conversations. It is important to take risks in terms of who to invite—playing it safe won't allow for
breakthrough moments.

Step 1.4. Schedule meeting. A data interpretation meeting typically
lasts from one and one-half to three hours, depending on the number of
placemats and participants. It is not recommended to go longer than three
hours; this type of meeting requires a lot of mental energy, attention to detail, and discussion—all of which may decrease over the duration of the
meeting. Typically, there's more energy and enthusiasm when discussing the
first few placemats, so it may be helpful to cover those placemats that would
benefit the most from stakeholder perspectives toward the front end of the
session.

While it is possible to conduct these meetings in an online setting, we
recommend conducting these meetings in person. Drawing from our experience, we feel that in-person facilitation promotes more active engagement
from participants and allows the facilitator to draw on his or her visual and
auditory senses, both of which we feel are critical in effective facilitation.

Step 1.5. Gather materials. In preparation for this meeting, the evaluator should:

• Print a set of placemats for each participant. It is not recommended to
  share the placemats with stakeholders ahead of time, unless the meeting
  will be conducted in an online setting.
• Have access to additional data and charts if needed (e.g., laptop files,
  printed tables, or appendices). For example, if investigating program participation rates, you may choose to display participation rates on the
  placemat by geographic location. During the meeting, a stakeholder may
  wonder aloud if participation rates differed by gender. With access to
  the cleaned data file on a nearby laptop, the evaluator can perform a
  quick cross-tabulation by gender and share findings with stakeholders
  immediately.

New Directions for Evaluation • DOI: 10.1002/ev

- Come prepared with a list of themes, based on the evaluator's initial interpretations.
- Bring highlighters and markers to encourage participants to scribble notes on the placemats during the meeting.
- Have access to a basic agenda—even if it's just in your head. It is helpful to think about how many minutes you should allocate to each placemat to ensure that all of them get covered during the meeting.

Phase 2. During the data interpretation meeting.   During the data interpretation meeting, the evaluator must play both a technical and adaptive role. Switching effectively between the two roles can be tricky and requires the ability to carefully balance both roles in an effort to empower stakeholders in the room to participate and take the collaborative conversation to the next level without dictating the end outcome of the meeting.

The evaluator will naturally read between the lines and form personal assessments of what the data are saying. These back-pocket explanations can be drawn on during the data interpretation meeting, but the evaluator must be open to amending—or altogether discarding—these personal hypotheses based on the stakeholders' conversations during the data interpretation meeting. The evaluator must be willing to allow the conversation to unfold naturally while balancing traditional evaluation duties such as answering methodological questions and traditional meeting facilitation duties such as keeping the discussion on track and on time.

Step 2.1. Explain the process. The evaluator starts by explaining the purpose of the meeting: "To share some data points from the evaluation and discuss what these data points may mean given your role, knowledge, and experience with the program/initiative. Together, we want to develop a mutual understanding of the information that has been collected for this evaluation."

Step 2.2. Lead a discussion of each placemat. The evaluator passes out hard copies of placemats one at a time; instructs the participants to skim each placemat; and encourages participants to underline, circle, and write down questions and comments. The evaluator guides group discussion by asking open-ended questions:

1. What do these data tell you?
2. What surprises you about these data?
3. What factors may explain some of the trends we are seeing?
4. Does this lead to any new questions?

The evaluator uses his or her adaptive capacities to modify the placemat structure and meeting format to a particular evaluation. Table 6.2 describes modifications based on the evaluation's focus, length, and impetus. As noted in the final column, this process works best when the evaluation is driven by a desire to learn rather than the need to justify funding.

Table 6.2. Adapting This Process for Different Evaluations

Impetus for Evaluation	Type of Evaluation	Structure of Placemats	Structure of Data Interpretation Meeting	Key Lessons/Insights
10-year retrospective of leadership development program	Requested by program staff wanting to learn more about program Results to be used to communicate with funders, but that was not the primary driver	Eight evaluation questions and eight corresponding placemats Contained quantitative survey data and qualitative interview data	One 3-hour in-person meeting Two evaluators and two program codirectors	• Codirectors were fully invested in the program and learning from the evaluation • Codirectors were honest with each other • Codirectors used this meeting as an opportunity to *learn* from the evaluation • Codirectors walked away feeling empowered
Two-year international fellowship program	Program funding being cut; evaluation an opportunity to prove program worth to funders	Three evaluation questions and three corresponding placemats Placemats contained data from interviews and surveys	One 3-hour in-person meeting Two evaluators and two codirectors	• Data placemats showed both positive and negative data • There were some instances in which stakeholders started casting blame for program shortcomings illustrated in placemats on others not present • Evaluator had to carefully navigate to keep conversations focused on contextual factors rather than calling out individual people • Evaluator had to facilitate the conversation to draw out the actual context behind the data trends; this was a challenge because stakeholders were more interested in shaping the story to attract more funders
10-year retrospective synthesis on advocacy and funding strategies related to human rights	Funder interested in compiling lessons to share with funders and advocates within the field	One placemat, highlighting six themes Placemats contained distillation of interview and survey themes	Due to power dynamics of key stakeholders, evaluator conducted three data interpretation meetings to ensure different voices and perspectives had the chance to weigh in	• Each data interpretation meeting yielded different interpretations of the data • Position within the field played a role in how stakeholders perceived and interpreted the data • Evaluator was able to integrate multiple viewpoints and perspectives into the final report, adding an additional layer of complexity and nuance

Phase 3. After the data interpretation meeting. After the data interpretation meeting, the evaluator returns to his or her office to conduct additional analyses and prepare the final deliverable.

Step 3.1. Conduct additional analyses as needed. Data interpretation meetings uncover opportunities for additional analysis, because the meeting participants' reflections provide a clearer understanding of the program's or initiative's context. Following the meeting, the evaluator revisits existing data to conduct analyses such as:

- Disaggregating participant subgroups or program cohorts based on meeting participants' ideas about how and why results varied across groups;
- Calculating inferential statistics to understand where meeting participants' sense of *practical significance* aligns with areas of *statistical significance*; and
- Triangulating findings across multiple data sources and time periods (e.g., reexamining focus group transcripts in light of meeting participants' insights about key survey patterns).

Data interpretation meetings also uncover questions that can be addressed in future performance management and evaluation efforts.

Step 3.2. Prepare the final deliverable. We suggest outlining the final report or presentation within a few days of the data interpretation meeting when meeting participants' conversations are easier to recall. In preparing the final deliverable, the evaluator would modify the charts from the data placemats (e.g., through shading choices and interpretive text as shown in Figure 6.3); design new charts (e.g., based on the additional analyses conducted in Step 3.1); and include meeting participants' stories, anecdotes, and hypotheses as to how and why findings occurred. This facilitation process adds an additional layer of insight and interpretation to the final deliverable that—without a data interpretation meeting—would not have been available.

Conclusion

In this chapter, we outlined a three-phase process for engaging stakeholders, building evaluation buy-in, and giving stakeholders space to think about and reflect upon findings. In Phase 1, the evaluator analyzes data and designs chart-based data placemats to display important patterns. In Phase 2, the evaluator facilitates a data interpretation meeting with program stakeholders. During the meeting, the evaluator asks stakeholders to interpret each of the charts and listens as stakeholders offer explanations for the results. In Phase 3, the evaluator conducts additional analyses and produces a final report or other deliverable.

The facilitation aspect of the data interpretation meeting is the hardest to gauge and prepare for ahead of time. Authenticity has helped us navigate

New Directions for Evaluation • DOI: 10.1002/ev

these interactions; being clear, open, and honest in communicating with stakeholders and identifying challenges goes a long way. In the example highlighted earlier in this chapter, we explained how "naming" the underlying tension within the room helped to lift the conversation to the next level. As a facilitator, it's not only important to be able to recognize negative currents that may be preventing conversation from naturally unfolding, but it's also important to be willing to take risks.

We have used this process in dozens of evaluation projects over the years. We continue to utilize this process because:

- The facilitator has an opportunity to create an environment where meeting participants can develop a shared understanding about the evaluation results, which increases both learning and buy-in;
- Insights gained from this process foster social equity, in which "those who give to the evaluation may benefit in return" (American Evaluation Association, 2004);
- Engaging those closest to the program or initiative ensures that findings are more valid and reflective of what is actually taking place than if the evaluator alone attempted to make meaning from the data, similar to *member check* techniques used in qualitative research;
- The data interpretation meeting itself is an opportunity to collect data— stakeholders share their reactions to the data, which allows the evaluator to present a well-rounded, comprehensive picture of the program or initiative in the final report; and
- When stakeholders participate in and better understand the information collected through an evaluation, the information is more likely to be used for program improvement.

References

American Evaluation Association. (2004). *Guiding principles for evaluators.* Retrieved from www.eval.org
American Evaluation Association. (2011). *Public statement on cultural competence in evaluation.* Fairhaven, MA: Author. Retrieved from www.eval.org
Cairo, A. (2013). *The functional art: An introduction to information graphics and visualization.* Berkeley, CA: New Riders.
Coffman, J., & Reed, E. (2009).*Unique methods in advocacy evaluation.* Retrieved from http://www.innonet.org/resources/files/Unique_Methods_Brief.pdf
Cousins, J. B., & Chouinard, J. A. (2012). *Participatory evaluation up close: An integration of research-based knowledge.* Charlotte, NC: Information Age.
Dean-Coffey, J. (2013). Graphic recording. In T. Azzam & S. Evergreen (Eds.), *Data Visualization, part 2. New Directions for Evaluation, 140,* 47–67.
Evergreen, S., & Metzner, C. (2013). Design principles for data visualization in evaluation. In T. Azzam & S. Evergreen (Eds.), *Data visualization for evaluation, part 2. New Directions for Evaluation, 140,* 5–20.

VEENA PANKAJ *is Director at Innovation Network, Inc. She is a skilled evaluator and facilitator and has over a decade of experience leading organizations through measurement and design processes.*

ANN K. EMERY *is an independent evaluation consultant who specializes in data analysis and visualization.*

NEW DIRECTIONS FOR EVALUATION • DOI: 10.1002/ev

Schwartz, A. (2016). Evaluating participatory facilitated conversations within the art of hosting framework. In R. S. Fierro, A. Schwartz, & D. H. Smart (Eds.), *Evaluation and Facilitation. New Directions for Evaluation, 149*, 95–106.

7

Evaluating Participatory Facilitated Conversations within the Art of Hosting Framework

Alissa Schwartz

Abstract

The Art of Hosting conversations that matter (AoH) is a practice framework for using participatory conversational structures and principles to foster meaningful conversation and collective intelligence. This chapter provides an overview of many of the conversational structures used in the AoH community, an explanation of the function of "harvesting" conversations, and a suggested framework for making decisions about evaluating participatory conversations. Evaluation of participatory conversations can focus on discerning the effects of a standalone conversation or a series of conversations that may involve the same or different groups of people meeting multiple times. There are three major approaches to evaluation—formative, summative, and developmental—that lend themselves well in conceptualizing the evaluation of AoH approaches, where the unit of analysis can be at multiple levels: individual, group, and systemic. The chapter concludes with the description of an evaluation of a World Café conversation facilitated at the 2014 American Evaluation Association conference in Denver, Colorado. © 2016 Wiley Periodicals, Inc., and the American Evaluation Association.

s with many chapters in this special issue, this one begins by defining facilitation as a set of guided interpersonal practices that help groups of people do something more easily. The focus of this chapter is on the evaluation of participatory conversational structures. Participatory conversational structures are a set of practices utilized by meeting facilitators to create structure for groups of people to converse about designated topics or questions. These structures are utilized in many kinds of facilitated group settings for a wide range of purposes. These include community and coalition building; organizational and system design, planning, and change; and evaluation and research. Very little has been written regarding the evaluation of participatory conversational structures.

The Art of Hosting conversations that matter (AoH) is a practice framework for using participatory conversational structures and principles to foster meaningful conversation and collective intelligence (Art of Hosting, 2014). This chapter provides an overview of many of the conversational structures used in the Art of Hosting community, an explanation of the function of "harvesting" conversations, and a suggested framework for making decisions about evaluating participatory conversations.

What Is the Art of Hosting?

The Art of Hosting conversations that matter is "a way of harnessing the collective wisdom and self-organizing capacity of groups of any size. . . . [It] blends a suite of powerful conversational processes to invite people to step in and take charge of the challenges facing them" (Art of Hosting, 2014). Such challenges include social, cultural, political, and economic issues facing groups of people within organizations, communities, and governing bodies. AoH approaches range in scale, from stand-alone 1- to 2-hour meetings, to multiday events, to long-term change processes that include multiple group meetings over time. AoH approaches are used in evaluation, strategy planning, and community and organizational building, as well as for other purposes.

Some of the AoH conversational structures used most often include Circle Practice, World Café, Open Space, and Pro Action Café. With the exception of ProAction Café, a hybrid structure utilizing aspects of World Café and Open Space that was developed by AoH practitioners Ria Baeck and Rainer Leoprechting (Baeck, 2010), these practices are also used by facilitators who are not affiliated with the AoH community. This chapter focuses on the evaluation of participatory conversations utilized within the AoH community because of the community's emphasis on both the importance of skillfully hosting participatory conversations as well as documenting them. Hosting is a set of practices that ensure the "comfort of participants, meaningful contributions, and collective intelligence" (see Fierro, Chapter 2, current NDE issue).

NEW DIRECTIONS FOR EVALUATION • DOI: 10.1002/ev

Table 7.1 provides a brief description of conversational structures used most often within the AoH community, their purpose, and additional resources for further information. Circle Practice, which involves an entire group engaging in nondialogic interaction where each person has the opportunity to share their thoughts and be heard by the entire group, is often used for community building and decision making. World Café, where a larger group is broken into smaller groups of three to five people and there are multiple rounds of conversation with interchanging partners, is used for collective visioning, planning, and coalescing of ideas. Open Space involves a group self-organizing into small groups centered on conversational topics of interest and is best used for project development. Pro Action Café, a hybrid of World Café and Open Space, involves small-group conversation on particular projects.

What Is Harvesting?

Along with developing practices to host conversations, AoH practitioners have an interest in documenting them. "Harvesting" is a set of practices comprising the documentation and synthesis of multiple points of view (Nissen & Corrigan, n.d.). Harvesting can include note taking, graphic recording, photography, and video, as well as the use of the arts (poetry, dance, music, theater, etc.) to capture the deep meaning and details of a conversation. Harvesting practices can be done by individuals engaged in conversations, nonparticipants listening in, and at the group level, during and after the conversations.

While "harvests" are typically shared with participants and other stakeholders following a conversation, the most useful and thoughtful ones are planned for and conceptualized before the conversation takes place. This is not unlike best practices in evaluation that recommend an evaluation be planned prior to the implementation of a project or program. Typical questions asked at the planning stage of harvesting conversations include:

- What is the purpose of the harvest? How will it be used?
- How will each phase of the conversational process be harvested?
- How can the harvest be an integral part of meaning-making for the group?
- Who will be doing the harvesting?
- Who will be using the harvest?
- What form(s) of "report" should the harvest take?

Clearly these questions are similar to some used when planning facilitated working sessions in evaluation projects (see Torres, Chapter 4, current NDE issue).

Table 7.1. Art of Hosting Conversational Structures

Structure	Purpose	Key Points	Resource
Circle Practice	Community building, decision making	• Participants sit in one circle • Guiding questions/topics are provided by the facilitator • One person speaks at a time • There is no "crosstalk" or dialog	www.peerspirit.com/gifts/PeerSpirit-Circle-Guidelines2010.pdf
World Café	Coalescing of ideas, planning, visioning	• Participants sit in small groups of 3–5 people • Guiding questions/topics are provided by the facilitator • Two or three rounds of interactive conversation are held where participants build on each other's ideas • Participants form different groups between each round	www.theworldcafe.com
Open Space	Project development, expansion of components of a project, issue, or set of concerns	• Conversational questions/topics are provided by participants • Participants choose among four roles: topic host, conversationalist, bumblebee (moves among more than one topic), and butterfly (chooses not to join a topic) • Topic groups can be of any size, based on participants' interest	www.openspaceworld.org
Pro Action Café	Involving group feedback and ideas in individual project development or to overcome specific challenges	• Conversational topics are provided by participants • Guiding questions are provided by facilitator • Participants choose among two roles: topic host or conversationalist • Topic hosts **workshop** a topic in small groups of 3–5 people • Two or three rounds of conversation are held where participants direct their comments to the topic host • Participants rotate among topic hosts	www.theworldcafecommunity.org/forum/topics/pro-action-cafe

NEW DIRECTIONS FOR EVALUATION • DOI: 10.1002/ev

Key Components for an Evaluation of Participatory Conversations

Evaluation of participatory conversations can focus on discerning the effects of a stand-alone conversation or a series of conversations that may involve the same or different groups of people meeting multiple times. An evaluation of participatory conversations can be undertaken for any number of purposes. It might be done to describe and analyze underlying patterns of event development in developmental evaluation, to document and understand individual and group processes in formative evaluation, or to demonstrate effectiveness in reaching particular outcomes in summative evaluation. In addition, the unit of analysis of an evaluation can be at multiple levels: individual, group, and systemic. Finally, many different data collection methodologies can be employed in service of the evaluation's purpose.

There is a great deal of interest in evaluating AoH conversational events, as evidenced by the conversational threads in their online community (Art of Hosting, n.d.). Interest in evaluation stems from demonstrating the effectiveness of AoH approaches to particular communities, organizations, and funding bodies, as well as the public at large. Research and evaluation of AoH approaches has largely focused on changes at the intrapersonal level, with studies describing participants' individual changes in knowledge, attitudes, and behavior after being trained and utilizing AoH approaches (Lang & Crawford, 2008; Sandfort, Stuber, & Quick, 2012; Success Works, 2011). Less attention has been given to evaluating the interpersonal or systemic impact of the conversations themselves.

Purpose of Evaluation

Patton (2010) categorizes evaluation approaches into three types: formative, summative, and developmental; these approaches lend themselves well in conceptualizing the evaluation of AoH approaches. Formative evaluation of an AoH event is concerned with understanding the internal mechanisms that make a participatory conversational event effective and focuses on its improvement. It can focus on understanding the processes used to move participants through a conversational event—from identification and invitation, to confirmation of participation, to participation and follow-up, as well as the processes utilized by the event's providers (or "hosting team" in AoH parlance), notably identification, recruitment, and training of facilitators, as well as planning and debriefing of the event.

Summative evaluation is concerned with the impact of a conversation, whether it involves changes in individuals, groups, or systems. There is increasing awareness throughout the AoH community that evaluating the results of participatory conversations would be particularly useful in helping to state the case for utilizing AoH approaches to external stakeholders, notably funders.

New Directions for Evaluation • DOI: 10.1002/ev

100 EVALUATION AND FACILITATION

Developmental evaluation focuses on understanding how a new initiative develops, from conceptualization to experimentation to pattern setting (Patton, 2010). Special attention is given to understanding what emerges from an initiative, with an appreciation for the complexity of interacting components. Developmental evaluation of an AoH event would focus on changes in perspectives, relationships, and outcomes of the event (Patton, 2010). Questions could focus, for example, on how the intent of the event emerged and how leadership and participant inclusion changed or evolved. These are questions that AoH event conveners are already generally quite sensitive to; however, systematic documentation and presentation of findings based on these kinds of questions are lacking within the field as a whole.

With its great emphasis on history and storytelling within the larger culture and strong theoretical alignment with the work of complexity science, complex adaptive systems, living systems, appreciative inquiry, and participatory and systemic action research (Burns, 2007; Chevalier & Buckles, 2013; Cooperrider & Whitney, 2005; Miller, 1995; Miller & Page, 2007; Waldrop, 1993), AoH conversations are well-suited for a developmental evaluation approach. Indeed, much of the informal conversation about evaluation on the AoH community's social media website is about the utility and application of this approach. To date, however, very little developmental evaluation of AoH events has been widely disseminated or published.

The Unit of Analysis for Evaluation

Change that occurs as the result of using AoH approaches can happen at three levels: intrapersonal, interpersonal, and systemic. The intrapersonal level is concerned with changes that happen for individuals, including changes in knowledge, attitudes, and behavior. Intrapersonal evaluations of an AoH event can focus on how individuals' participation shifts over time, the generation of novel and appropriate ideas or solutions, or individuals' receptivity to using participatory conversational structures to work collectively on future issues.

The interpersonal level is concerned with changes that happen between participants and includes changes in knowledge, attitudes, and behavior at the group level. While aggregation of individual-level data can yield an approximation of what occurred interpersonally, it doesn't speak to changes that occurred for the group as a whole. An evaluation of an AoH event at the interpersonal level can include, for example, an examination of the group dynamics among participants and use of power in decision making, conflict resolution, and strategizing.

The systemic level of evaluation of an AoH event is concerned with changes that happen in a larger environment as a result of the conversations that occurred. This is, by far, the most difficult kind of evaluation to undertake and requires considerable planning and resources to accomplish.

Contextual changes happening beyond the actual AoH event can include changes in organizational and systemic meeting practices, structure, policy, and programs. Burns's (2007) work on systemic action research is aligned with this approach, as are approaches that consider collective impact (Kramer & Kania, 2013).

Data Collection Methods

In Table 7.2, I propose several data collection methods to use when evaluating participatory conversations, a suggested purpose for each given method, as well as its strengths and challenges. These methods can be put to various evaluative purposes, whether it is formative, summative, or developmental. Some methods lend themselves better to different units of analysis, and that is indicated as well. It is by no means exhaustive and offers a beginning point for thinking about the methods that can be used to conduct the evaluation of participatory conversations.

For example, pre- and postconversational data collection activities focused on intrapersonal impact are relatively easy to conduct, but generally rely on predetermined questions and may not yield rich, nuanced information. While it may be more intrusive to insert an evaluation-related question into the conversational event itself, where the priority in use of time is focused on delving into the topics of importance to a group rather than evaluation of the process itself, the intrapersonal data may be richer, although confidentiality can be compromised. Content analysis and concept mapping, which tap into interpersonal impact, both require conversational harvests that are thorough and detailed enough to yield meaningful data for analysis. Both behavioral observation and network mapping, which can tap into interpersonal and to some extent systemic impact, require extensive preplanning to determine observational or network components as well as an ability to observe and note emerging, unexpected behaviors and interactions. While conducting postconversation individual or group interviews at a later time is the least intrusive with regard to the actual conversational event and yields the richest, most nuanced data with regard to systemic impact, it also requires a great deal of additional resources to engage in effectively.

Case Example: Evaluation of a World Café Conversation about Evaluation

The ability to facilitate group processes and conversations is an important skill for evaluators, whether they are working internally or externally with an organization. Some evaluation frameworks, notably empowerment, transformative, and collaborative ones (Fetterman & Wandersman, 2005; Mertens, 2009; O'Sullivan, 2004) place particular emphasis on ensuring collective input of multiple stakeholders at various stages of an evaluation

New Directions for Evaluation • DOI: 10.1002/ev

Table 7.2. Evaluation Methods for Participatory Conversations

Data Collection Method	Unit of Analysis	Purpose	Example(s)	Strengths	Challenges
Pre- and Postconversation activities or surveys	Intrapersonal	Determine change in participants' levels of confidence in producing meaningful solutions (and other impacts) prior to and following conversations (summative)	• A show of hands prior to and following conversations • Paper/online surveys • Human sliding scale: Asking participants to physically align themselves in a room based on a question	• Allows data to be collected from all participants • Data can be collected at individual or group level	• Questions are predetermined • Allows little opportunity to gain information about what may emerge as a result of the conversation • Activities may not allow for anonymous responses
Incorporating an evaluation-related question in the facilitated conversation	Intrapersonal	Determine participants' sense of effectiveness of utilizing conversational methods and/or the ideas they have generated (summative)	• One word/phrase check out • Final round of conversation in World Café having an evaluative component	• Highly interactive • Allows the capture of many perspectives • Allows for the emergence of evaluation questions	• Participants may influence each other during the conversation; issues of confidentiality may be compromised
Content Analysis, Concept Mapping	Interpersonal	Determine relationship between original intent of conversation, conversational questions/topics, and responses generated (developmental)	• Examination of themes across documentation (notes, graphic recording, photos, videos, etc.) produced during conversations	• Allows review of existing documents for specific information	• Content and availability of documents across conversations may vary too much or be unavailable in some cases

(Continued)

Table 7.2. Continued

Data Collection Method	Unit of Analysis	Purpose	Example(s)	Strengths	Challenges
Observation	Interpersonal	Determine quality of interaction among participants, including differentials in power (formative)	• Demographic analysis of conversational hosts for Open Space and Pro Action Café	• Allows evaluator to analyze complex interactions during participatory conversations	• Requires extensive planning concerning what to look for • The conversation that emerges may not correspond to the observation design of the facilitator
Network Mapping	Interpersonal Systemic	Determine strength and number of ties among participants during conversations (formative)	• Mapping interactions within a conversation	• Allows evaluator to analyze complex subgroup dynamics within the conversation	• May require multiple evaluators/facilitators to collect data on multiple simultaneous conversations
Postconversation Interviews and Group Conversations	Systemic	Determine impact of conversations beyond event (summative)	• Interviewing Open Space and Pro Action Café hosts to learn about the impact of conversations on subsequent activity and relationships • Meeting with participants to do the same	• Allows participants freedom to expand beyond what was already known and discussed and ask about what is unknown • Can allow for anonymous responses	• Time needed for data collection and for analysis

process. Evaluators utilizing qualitative forms of data collection, such as focus groups, also need strong group facilitation skills.

AoH approaches lend themselves particularly well to these evaluation frameworks and approaches and can also be used in other settings. I have used the World Café process for data collection and found that it yields higher levels of interactivity when compared to focus groups. Whereas focus groups require active facilitation to moderate the disparate levels of input from participants, a World Café conversation is largely self-moderated and focused within small groups of three to five people. With focus groups, comments are often directed toward the facilitator, who serves as a de facto communication hub. With World Café, each table of conversation is inwardly focused. Synthesis of findings is a natural part of the World Café process as well, when each small group reports key points at the end of a conversational round. AoH approaches can also lend themselves well to other phases of an evaluation process, from collectively developing research questions and an evaluation design to analyzing findings to determining how to use evaluation results going forward.

At the 2014 American Evaluation Association's annual conference in Denver, Colorado, Rita S. Fierro, Dawn Hanson Smart, and I cofacilitated a World Café conversation. The theme of the conference was Visionary Evaluation for a Sustainable, Equitable Future. To help unpack this theme and give voice to the myriad of ideas, opinions, and experiences present at the conference, we designed a community conversation with two rounds of questions:

1. What does a sustainable, equitable world look like to you?
2. How can evaluation support that vision?

To evaluate the outcome of the conversation at the intrapersonal level, we conducted a pretest, posttest survey with just one open-ended question to get a sense of what participants had hoped to gain and what they actually gained from talking with one another. We did this by asking participants to write a word or short phrase on a Post-it note prior to engaging in the first round of conversation and at the end of the process.

Approximately 20 people participated in the World Café; however, some joined the session in the middle of the first round of conversation or later. We were able to collect 13 pretest responses and 18 posttest ones. Responses were grouped together according to similar themes.

Five kinds of desired gains were present in the pretest responses. Nearly half ($n = 6$; 46%) of the responses were evaluation related, falling into two themes: (a) exploring the conference's theme, and (b) generally learning more about evaluation. Nearly a quarter ($n = 3$, 23%) of participants were looking for inspiration and insight from the conversation, and the remaining participants were hoping to gain interpersonal connection ($n = 2$, 15%) or learn more about the World Café process itself ($n = 2$, 15%).

Four kinds of actualized gains were reported in the posttest responses. More than half ($n = 11$, 61%) of the responses were evaluation related and generally focused on developing a broader conceptualization of the role of evaluation in supporting a sustainable, equitable world. In particular, the concept of evaluators engaging in (a) advocacy and action, (b) making things visible, and (c) storytelling came up several times. More than a quarter ($n = 5$, 28%) of participants reported gaining inspiration and insight, and the remaining two participants (11%) reported gains in interpersonal connection and a better understanding of the concept of sustainability.

While there is no way to ascertain that the World Café method we used resulted in greater personal gains in comparison to using an alternative method to generate ideas (e.g., a focus group), we three facilitators certainly noted the high level of involvement around each table, with participants leaning in, taking notes together, nodding heads, and developing a collective vision. AoH methods demand that participants, rather than the facilitator, take responsibility for the direction of a conversation. It is not surprising, then, that participants reported high levels of new thinking and interpersonal connection.

This simple pretest, posttest evaluation confirmed that the questions we used during our World Café yielded new insight and understanding for participants with regard to the role of evaluators in a sustainable, equitable world. It is interesting to note that no participants mentioned they had actually learned more about the World Café process itself. While this was not a stated purpose of the session, some participants did express this as an interest in their pretest responses. This could mean that everyone was so engaged with the topic being discussed that they lost sight of their original primary interest in learning more about the methods used to elicit that participation.

In conclusion, while many AoH training events have been evaluated, notably to detect changes at the individual and interpersonal levels, there are fewer publicly available studies of the impact of participatory conversational structures outside of training settings, especially with regard to impact at the systems level. This chapter provides a conceptual framework to help future evaluators of participatory conversational processes determine what kind of evaluation they would like to undertake (formative, summative, developmental) at what unit of analysis (individual, group, system), with an array of suggested data collection methodologies.

References

Baeck, R. (2010). Pro Action Café. Retrieved October 31, 2015 from http://artofhosting .ning.com/page/core-art-of-hosting-practices

Burns, D. (2007). *Systemic action research: A strategy for whole system change.* Bristol, UK: The Policy Press.

Chevalier, D., & Buckles, J. (2013). *Participatory action research: Theory and methods for engaged inquiry.* New York, NY: Routledge.

Art of Hosting. (2014). *What is the art of hosting conversations that matter?* Retrieved from http://www.artofhosting.org/what-is-aoh/http://www.artofhosting.org/

Art of Hosting. (n.d.). *Conversation forum.* Retrieved September 23, 2014, from http://artofhosting.ning.com/forum

Cooperrider, D., & Whitney, D. (2005). *Appreciative inquiry: A positive revolution in change.* San Francisco, CA: Berrett-Koehler.

Fetterman, D., & Wandersman, A. (2005). *Empowerment evaluation principles in practice.* New York, NY: Guilford Press.

Kramer, J., & Kania, M. (2013, January 21). Embracing emergence: How collective impact addresses complexity. *Stanford Social Innovation Review.*

Lang, D., & Crawford, D. (2008, July). *Evaluation of the Art of Hosting trainings final report.* Columbus Medical Association Foundation. Retrieved from http://artofhosting.ning.com/page/research-papers

Mertens, D. (2009). *Transformative research and evaluation.* New York, NY: Guilford Press.

Miller, J. (1995). *Living systems.* Boulder: University of Colorado Press.

Miller, J., & Page, S. (2007). *Complex adaptive systems: An introduction to computational models of social life.* Princeton, NJ: Princeton University Press.

Nissen, M., & Corrigan, C. (n.d.). *The art of harvesting* (3rd ed.). Silkeborg, Denmark: InterChange. Retrieved from http://www.interchange.dk/practices/artofharvesting

O'Sullivan, R. (2004). *Practicing evaluation: A collaborative approach.* Thousand Oaks, CA: Sage.

Patton, M. (2010). *Developmental evaluation: Applying complexity concepts to enhance innovation and use.* New York, NY: Guilford Press.

Sandfort, J., Stuber, N., & Quick, K. (2012, July). *Practicing the Art of Hosting: Exploring what Art of Hosting and Harvesting workshop participants understand and do.* Center for Integrative Leadership, Humphrey School, University of Minnesota. Retrieved from http://www.leadership.umn.edu/education/documents/PractingtheArtofHostingReport.pdf

Success Works. (2011, October). *Evaluation of the Art of Hosting and Harvesting conversations that matter success works conferences 2009–2011.* Carlton, Australia: Success Works. Retrieved from http://api.ning.com/files/djUuyfw7gFKz1yI05CRqAvwVmjPvMNGsBG0∗GarVsITdMOZEUxlFtUHdDJW∗DWhAtXvL1w62Isb4vtGgW∗oWFxXglPCRB∗I3/AoHSuccessWorksEvaluationReport2011.pdf

Waldrop, M. (1993). *Complexity: The emerging science at the edge of order and chaos.* New York, NY: Simon & Schuster.

ALISSA SCHWARTZ, MSW, PhD, is an independent organizational consultant with a practice in participatory facilitation, program evaluation, leadership development, and strategy planning. You can learn more about her work from her website: www.solidfireconsulting.com

NEW DIRECTIONS FOR EVALUATION • DOI: 10.1002/ev

Dart, J., & Roberts, M. (2016). Invisible and unbound? The challenge and practice of evaluating embedded facilitation. In R. S. Fierro, A. Schwartz, & D. H. Smart (Eds.), *Evaluation and Facilitation. New Directions for Evaluation, 149,* 107–120.

8

Invisible and Unbound? The Challenge and Practice of Evaluating Embedded Facilitation

Jessica Dart, Megan Roberts

Abstract

With the movement in Australia toward smaller government, there is a growing emphasis on how to allocate scarce resources efficiently. In this tighter financial climate, placement of facilitators into programs and services offers a promise of achieving more with less. As a result there are a plethora of government and nongovernment programs that make use of facilitators directly funded by programs. Despite the appeal of using facilitators, little attention has been paid to how best to evaluate the facilitation component of programs. The literature on the nature of facilitation points to difficulties in attributing outcomes to facilitation and the importance of understanding the intent. We use a case study of the past 15 years of evaluating Landcare programs in Australia to explore the challenges further and offer practical ideas for any evaluators faced with the prospect of evaluating a program that has a facilitative element. © 2016 Wiley Periodicals, Inc., and the American Evaluation Association.

With a movement in Australia toward smaller government, there is a growing emphasis on how to achieve more with less. Partnerships with community and increased agency collaboration have been explored by government, and need the support of facilitators. In a tighter financial climate, facilitators offer the promise of "knitting together"

NEW DIRECTIONS FOR EVALUATION, no. 149, Spring 2016 © 2016 Wiley Periodicals, Inc., and the American Evaluation Association. Published online in Wiley Online Library (wileyonlinelibrary.com) • DOI: 10.1002/ev.20183 the reduced services offered to communities or of mobilizing communities to take action themselves and leverage scarce resources.

Facilitation, while being broadly defined as "making (an action or process) easy or easier" (Oxford English Dictionary, 2010), may take on many different forms. A distinction necessary for framing our discussion here is between a facilitated process as a *standalone intervention* (often in a workshop setting) (see Schwartz, Chapter 7, current NDE issue), versus placement of facilitators in a community or agency setting to serve as a *mechanism within* a program. In this article we focus on the latter. For ease of language, we refer to this as "embedded facilitation" to distinguish it from *standalone* facilitated processes or workshops.

Programs with embedded facilitation tend to fall into two types: programs that aim to mobilize people to take action themselves, and service delivery programs that use facilitators to help better connect isolated or marginalized communities to services. Some programs make use of both types. In both instances, a key feature of the work of facilitators is that they are not necessarily technical experts. Instead, they work to connect, broker, support, empower, and involve people in pursuing their own agendas. Examples of programs that make strong use of facilitators are widely spread and span many community-based interventions including health, education, natural resource management, international development, and more. In our experience as evaluation and facilitation practitioners, community facilitators often work with local communities, but can also operate between regional or national agencies, as well as inside organizations. In Australia, there has been a long tradition of using community facilitators in natural resource management programs. In these programs, facilitators are placed in a full-time capacity in communities and agencies to support community groups and help connect individuals, groups, and agencies.

Within this scope, in this article we explore the dilemmas and possibilities of evaluating facilitation as a mechanism that is embedded within a broader program and evaluated as one component of a more comprehensive program evaluation. As there is no cohesive discourse on evaluating embedded facilitation, we first examine several bodies of literature that help inform the ideas we present in this article, including the literature on facilitation in general and the dispersed body of literature on evaluating programs that make strong use of facilitation. We then draw some lessons from kindred processes such as evaluating networks and community engagement (by which we refer to processes that involve the public in identifying issues or use public input to make decisions). Following the literature review, we present a case study of the past 15 years of evaluating Landcare programs in Australia. Landcare is a state-sponsored, community-driven natural resource management intervention that draws on government-funded facilitators. It employs facilitators who create opportunities for farmers to be involved in conservation initiatives of their land and in collaboration with other land managers. We use this case study as an example of embedded facilitation to explore the challenges encountered in evaluating such programs. Finally, we bring together lessons from the literature with those from Australian practice to draw out some possible solutions and directions for how best to evaluate embedded facilitation.

What Can Be Learned From Existing Literature?

A review of literature reveals that there is no cohesive body of discourse on evaluating embedded facilitation. Instead there are several bodies of literature that help inform our arguments, but do not address it directly. These include literature on:

- Facilitation itself, how it is defined, and what makes good facilitation
- The dilemmas encountered when evaluating kindred embedded processes such as engagement and networks
- How to evaluate programs that include high use of facilitation with the community such as: health, natural resource management, and international development

A summary of these themes is presented next.

Literature on Facilitation Itself, How It Is Defined, and What Makes Good Facilitation

Much of the literature about evaluating facilitation relates to facilitated processes as a *standalone intervention* (e.g., often in a workshop setting) (see Schwartz, Chapter 7, current NDE issue). Authors in this issue, and others, have noted that good facilitation involves planning, managing group processes, keeping participants safe, and enabling groups to reach their own decisions (Hogan, 2002; International Association of Facilitators, 2006). This is useful; however, it is mostly oriented toward facilitation in a workshop setting rather than the more unbounded and continuous nature of the work of a community-based facilitator. Relating to the latter, the notions of good facilitation may stretch to networking, mobilization, motivating, catalyzing, and brokering, and is largely ongoing and relational.

Literature About the Challenges of Evaluating Kindred Embedded Processes Such as Evaluating Networks and Engagement

Evaluating Networks Approaches. Benjamin and Greene (2009) pose a series of dilemmas around evaluands that are not programmatically defined or bounded, but consist of public and private actors collaborating across organizational, sectoral, and geographic boundaries. The challenges resonate with evaluations of embedded facilitation, particularly programs that work at regional or national scales of governance but seek local, place-based involvement. The challenges cited by Benjamin and

Greene (2009) include the way the evaluand was constantly refined, that the evaluand was more opportunistic and emergent than programmatic, and that project boundaries were unclear. This is certainly the case for much embedded evaluation, where facilitators work in very opportunistic and variable ways. Benjamin and Greene (2009) remind us that in evaluability assessment, evaluands such as these would not be deemed sufficiently mature to adequately assess their effectiveness (Shadish, Cook, & Leviton, 1991). They recommend that other frameworks such as social network analysis may form a more appropriate basis to guide evaluations and that, in this circumstance, evaluators should assume the role of "network mappers."

Evaluating Community Engagement. Like embedded facilitation, community engagement is a pivotal part of many programs and policies (and possibly even more widespread than embedded facilitation). By community engagement, we refer to processes that involve the public in identifying issues or decisions and use public input to make decisions. While the logic of evaluating engagement is entirely consistent with that of program evaluation more broadly, like embedded facilitation, there are some challenges related to the nature of the process of engagement (Carson, Twyford, & Meek, 2005). In particular, like facilitation, when engagement goes well, it is almost invisible; people notice it more easily when it is done badly and can result in outrage. Additionally, while it is challenging to engage communities in the first instance, it can be doubly difficult to engage them a second time for evaluation purposes. Very easily, they can suffer from what is known as "engagement fatigue" (Carson et al., 2005). Thus, an important point for evaluating both engagement and embedded facilitation is that gathering feedback from community members is likely to be insufficient due to the invisible nature of the process and due to engagement fatigue.

Literature on Evaluating Programs With a Significant Facilitation Component

There is a wide range of gray literature guiding practitioners how to evaluate community development, community health programs, and participatory international development. This comes in the forms of manuals, online resources, books, and papers (see, for example, Ayers, Anderson, Pradhan, & Rossing, 2012; Kaufman, Ozawa, & Shmueli, 2014; Otoo, Agapitova, & Behrens, 2009; UNESCO, 2009). A considerable amount of this guidance covers programs that include community facilitators, but not all. While a thorough analysis of this massive body of literature was not conducted here, in our limited review we found only a few examples of program evaluations that specifically pay attention to how to evaluate the role of the facilitator. Instead the guidance focuses more on how to measure and report on the achievements of the community, and the extent to which specific program goals have been reached.

New Directions for Evaluation • DOI: 10.1002/ev

We found few published evaluations of the actual effectiveness or impact of facilitation as a mechanism within community programs. There are some exceptions, particularly from the field of international development. For example, an evaluation of a neonatal program in Vietnam looked at the difference in outcomes for self-help groups that had a facilitator and those that did not have a facilitator (Eriksson, 2012). The groups with facilitators showed much lower neonatal death rates. In another example, Oxfam (Hughes & Hutchins, 2011) evaluated its Fair Play campaign, which acts as a facilitator, bringing together over 200 civil society partners to work in coalition on existing campaigns using "process tracing" to enable assessment of whether interim outcomes that signal progress toward desired outcomes were occurring. This involved constructing a theory of change and seeking plausible causal explanations for the outcomes. The evaluation found that many of the expected interim outcomes were achieved and could be plausibly associated with the facilitation, yet many of the outcomes of interest were not achieved.

Looking at published evaluations and the guidance literature, it appears that embedded facilitation displays approximately the same types of issues and possibilities as many types of programs operating in complex settings that strive to achieve social, economic, or environmental outcomes (Eriksson, 2012; Hughes & Hutchins, 2011). However, the salient points of difference for inquiry into embedded facilitation are that the role of the facilitator is somewhat "invisible" and that gathering feedback from community members is likely to be insufficient (Colliver, 2011). This is consistent with literature on evaluating engagement. It can be hard to disentangle the results of the facilitation from the work of various other factors—its opportunistic, emergent, and context-specific nature makes it hard to define and pin down the outcomes (which is consistent with literature about evaluating networks).

The Case of Landcare in Australia

In Australia there has been a strong tradition of placing facilitators in communities to support community action and community groups involved in natural resource management (Fenton, 2007; Hassall & Associates, 2003; Raetz, 2012; URS Australia, 2001). One of the most well-known and frequently evaluated is the Landcare program. We use Landcare as an example to explore some of the dilemmas and possible solutions for evaluating embedded facilitation.

The Landcare program in Australia is an example of an iterative program that has facilitation at the heart of all levels of delivery: at national, state government scales, at the regional or catchment scale, and at the landscape scale. The program emerged in the state of Victoria during 1986 and was replicated across Australia as a model for effective community action to manage land degradation and more sustainable land use (Campbell,

1989; Lockie & Vanclay, 2006). Landcare is often described as both a state-sponsored public participation program and a grassroots social movement. Both descriptions emphasize an approach to environmental management based on self-help, cooperation, and planning (Bailey, 2006). Landcare began and has continued to oscillate between being both a state-sponsored and community-driven collaboration between rural (and increasingly, urban and peri-urban) citizens working together to achieve environmental management outcomes within their "catchment" or "watershed" (Lockie & Vanclay, 2006). To encourage community participation in Landcare, for over two decades state and federal governments in Australia have invested in facilitation and coordination as a key influencing activity (Curtis & Sample, 2010; Hassall & Associates, 2009; Raetz, 2012; URS Australia, 2001). A central role of Landcare facilitators is to support community Landcare groups and networks by connecting them to other groups, networks, and agencies, as well as encouraging and empowering community members to pursue their own agendas around managing land. They often also act as an interface between community members and agencies. At its peak in 2003, there were 417 Landcare facilitators in Australia and 685 facilitators across different natural resource management programs, costing around AU$32.31 million. In 2011, community groups received over 50% of the federal funding for natural resource management (Hassall & Associates, 2003).

Community and government alike perceived Landcare as a program about supporting community identification, prioritization, and ownership of conservation activity (Bailey, 2006). Since its inception in 1986, Landcare still persists today as both an informal social movement and as formal associations, networks, and government-funded programs. At its root, it relies on facilitation and coordination.

Evaluation of Landcare

Landcare has, both directly and indirectly, been subject to numerous evaluations at the local, state, and national level (see, for example, Curtis, Robertson, & Race, 1998; Ewing, 2006; Grant & Curtis, 2004; Hassall & Associates, 2003; Raetz, 2012; Roberts, 1998; Walker, 1998). Evaluations have focused on a wide range of topics from concentrating on the natural resource management outcomes to the social capital outcomes.

The nature of Landcare as an inherently facilitative program has made it a challenging program to evaluate. This has been explored for several decades. The literature cites several outstanding challenges and solutions around evaluating the facilitated element of Landcare. In the paragraphs below, we present four key challenges to evaluating embedded facilitation in Landcare. The discussion of each challenge commences with an exhibit box which summarizes the key challenge and offers potential practices to address this challenge.

Exhibit 8.1.

Key Challenge 1: Determining the intent of embedded facilitation and clarifying the key mechanisms to influence change: On what basis should success be pegged?
Practice 1: Map out the theory of change to help gain consensus about how embedded facilitation leads to outcomes of interest, but be ready to redefine it over time as the intervention changes.

Determining the intent of Landcare, including its fundamental component of embedded facilitation, has long been contested and varies from program to program and between different contexts (e.g., see Campbell, 2006; Curtis & Lockwood, 2000; Lockie & Vanclay, 2006). Some see the ultimate outcomes in terms of reduction of environmental risks (e.g., Curtis & De Lacy, 2006, explore this), while others stress that the ultimate outcomes be expressed as social outcomes—such as community engagement in the environment (Ewing, 2006).

In several cases, evaluations have made attempts to clarify the underpinning theory of change for Landcare (Dart & McGarry, 2006; Hassall & Associates, 2003; Raetz, 2012). While no universal model has ever been agreed on (and is unlikely to do so), there are examples where this has been beneficial for specific locations and programs. For example, the Regional Landcare Program in Victoria developed a theory of change model

Figure 8.1. Summary Logic of Landcare

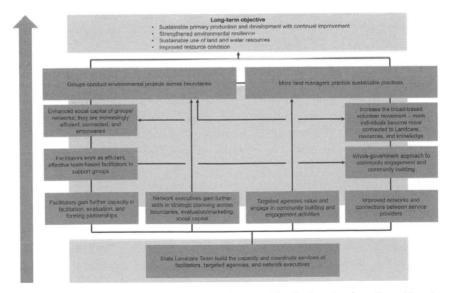

(Adapted from Dart and McGarry 2006, p. 7, and prepared for the State Landcare Team, Victoria, 2006)

and found this helpful in defining key evaluation questions and developing methods that addressed outcomes more closely connected to their work (Dart & McGarry, 2006). Interestingly, even in this program, the logic model was revised four times between the period of 2002 and 2008. Reasons for modification included changing policies and changes in key executives who had differing views on the desired outcomes of the program. Figure 8.1 shows the program logic model as it was in 2006. The program team at this time was able to illustrate using program theory how facilitators enhanced the social capital of groups, who in turn became increasingly efficient, connected, and empowered. As a result, the program delivered more environmental projects across farm boundaries. In particular, unpacking the program theory enabled the identification of "interim outcomes," which played an important role in establishing a causal relationship between facilitation and the achievement of end-outcomes. The Regional Landcare Program in Victoria program used theory-based evaluation to demonstrate its worth to a sufficient extent, making it one of the few programs that maintained funding for facilitators at the state level (Dart & McGarry, 2006).

Exhibit 8.2.

Key Challenge 2: Engagement fatigue from embedded facilitation and evaluation and the importance of the way in which evaluation is conducted.
Practice 2: Focus on where the group stands in relation to their own goals. Global assessment scales with accessible language can be useful. Effective approaches include using participatory evaluation that is entwined in what the participants are interested in doing.

Embedded facilitation, in the case of Landcare, relies on leveraging the voluntary time of the community members who join groups, discuss activities, and manage networks. Networks are often formed when multiple Landcare groups organize to form larger coalitions and are overseen by a voluntary management committee and assisted by an employed facilitator. For these community volunteers, evaluation can seem intrusive and a waste of precious time: "For management committees of networks, staff and volunteer time was too precious to waste on talk: Networks would only participate if they could set the agenda and work on a pressing development task" (Colliver, 2011, p. 11). In this context, it would be unwise to add further "burden" without clear and explicit intent of evaluation activities and "piggy-backing" on existing work being done. In this instance, action research (intended to evaluate and improve natural resource management governance) was found as a useful approach to avoid engagement fatigue because it allowed Landcare networks to set their own agenda and use time generating data to work on tasks of their choosing (Colliver, 2011).

The nature of a program with a high degree of community ownership calls for evaluation approaches that reinforce this ownership without adding further burden on participants. One example of a widely adopted tool for this purpose was the "group health scale" (described further in Dart & McGarry, 2006). This is a basic five-point global assessment scale that describes five levels of "how good" a Landcare group is. Each level describes a group at different stages of group health from "just hanging in there" to "trail blazing." Each level of the scale includes a description of a group and a colloquial title. To score themselves, groups choose a level that best fits how they see themselves at a point in time, and this is compared at regular annual intervals. The benefit of this tool is that it was very easy to score— just requiring groups to note where they are today, and where they wish to be in the future—but it is also useful to groups because it allows them to clarify with the facilitator the type of support they may need, and how active they wish to be (Dart & McGarry, 2006).

Where Landcare is being evaluated, some aspects of embedded facilitation is being evaluated (whether explicitly or not). Linked to the need to reduce engagement fatigue is the need for appropriate evaluation process. As with most evaluation contexts, evaluations or any other forms of social inquiry in the Landcare context need to be culturally competent and contextually driven, as well as appropriate to the diversity of culture, language, and social practices of Landcare communities in rural and regional Australia (Compton & Beeton, 2012). Landcare operates in a range of cultural contexts, including embracing Aboriginal communities and groups of ethnically diverse communities and a whole range of farming families, communities, and businesses (Campbell, 2006). To this end, when evaluating embedded facilitation, as with other kinds of evaluands, there are clear reasons to account for this context and acknowledge power relationships embedded in language, status, and bureaucracy.

Exhibit 8.3.

Key challenge 3: Dealing with the unbounded network aspects of Landcare.
Practice 3: Ensure that interim outcomes are considered, including the reach of networks. Simple approaches to mapping social networks can be useful here, as well as more complex evaluations of networks.

Evaluating the role of facilitators who work directly with Landcare groups is somewhat more visible and evaluable than the work of facilitators who broker relationships and catalyze action at the regional or national level. This is because improved performance of a Landcare group can be directly linked back to the work of the facilitator, whereas the work of facilitators outside of Landcare groups is more "unbound"—it is opportunistic, emergent, and context-specific and occurs between multiple agencies and networks. This type of work is particularly hard to define and it is also hard to trace its impact. This issue corresponds closely with challenges seen in trying to evaluate network approaches (Benjamin & Greene, 2009; Taylor, Plastrik, Coffman, & Whatley, 2014). The issue is the evaluand is extremely hard to define and varies widely from context to context, with facilitators building on a wider range of opportunities and leveraging from diverse relationships (see, for example, Hassall & Associates, 2003). What seems to be important here is to use evaluation approaches that are able to document the value of the connections between people (e.g., networks and social capital) to show the outcomes of Landcare facilitators across bureaucratic scales (Compton & Beeton, 2012; Sobels, Curtis, & Lockie, 2001).

In the case study of the Landcare program in Victoria, the program logic revealed that a central role of the regional facilitators was to improve the connections between different agencies and to empower existing Landcare groups to take action. These "interim" outcomes are several steps removed from the actual on-ground impacts. As these intermediate outcomes are likely to be relational and emergent, specific methods of evaluation that can explore changes in relationships and collaboration, such as social network mapping, can be useful (Taylor et al., 2014). There is considerable work underway in exploring approaches to evaluation of networks themselves. Some of this work may offer insights into understanding how to evaluate the more "unbound" aspects of embedded facilitation, from understanding the role of networks as part of broader theories of change to mapping and analyzing networks evaluatively (Taylor et al., 2014). The "unbound" aspects of Landcare facilitators constitute a large part of their work—so finding ways to evaluate this mechanism is important. This is also relevant for many other programs that may adopt an embedded facilitation model. With a move toward smaller government in Australia (and in several other countries), there may well be a continued trend toward programs that aim to "do more with less" by connecting together existing services and mobilizing communities to set their own agenda and solve problems.

Exhibit 8.4.

Key challenge 4: Invisibility factor of good facilitation and the challenge of attribution. **Practice 4:** If the evaluation aims to shoot for making rigorous claims about attribution, then we suggest looking to some of the qualitative/mixed-method approaches to establishing causality such as Process Tracing, General Elimination Methodology, Contribution Analysis, and Collaborative Outcomes Reporting.

Facilitation in Landcare is just one element in a complex dynamic of community volunteerism, agency, existing assets and groups, networks, and environmental context. When a community Landcare group does great work, the focus tends to be on the group's efforts. Conversely, the facilitator's role is to support from the background, to create space for others to flourish. As a result, their influence is not always visible—both to beneficiaries and evaluators (Colliver, 2011; Ewing, 2006). This raises questions of attribution. No evaluations were found of Landcare that used experimental or quasi-experimental approaches to prove the impact of facilitation. This is where program theory and interim outcomes play an important role in providing evidence of a causal relationship between the facilitation and the outcomes of interest. On this basis there does appear to be a fairly convincing portfolio of evidence from social research and evaluations to suggest facilitation, at least at the Landcare group level, is a vital aspect of Landcare (Bailey, 2006; Colliver, 2011; Compton & Beeton, 2012; Ewing, 2006; Fenton, 2007). Historic records show that where government did not support Landcare facilitators, overall participation in groups declined (Hassall & Associates, 2003). Evaluators appear to have had more trouble making a strong case for attributing facilitation to outcomes of interest with regard to the more unbounded work of facilitators and coordinators who operate at the postgroup level.

Some other Landcare evaluations used Collaborative Outcomes Reporting (also known as Performance Story Reporting), an approach that draws from Mayne's (2001) contribution analysis, but also takes a participatory and inclusive approach (Dart, 2008; Dart & Roberts, 2014). As well as taking a program theory approach, and using multiple lines of evidence, it uses expert panels to discuss and explore what would have happened without the program (the counterfactual) and provide expert opinion on whether the causal claims are plausible. There are several instances where this approach has been employed to evaluate Landcare investments in Australia (see, for example, East Gippsland Catchment Management Authority, 2010; Goulburn Broken Catchment Management Authority, 2010). While those examples do not explicitly evaluate the facilitative aspects of the Landcare investments in question, the approach would be well-adapted for incorporating specific reference to evaluating the influence of embedded facilitation.

If those evaluating Landcare do aim to make a strong case for attribution, they would be well served by using some of the more in-depth qualitative/mixed approaches to establishing causality as described by the International Initiative for Impact Evaluation (3ie) in White & Phillips (2012). These include Process Tracing, an approach to causal inference that uses a case-based method and focuses on the use of clues within a case (as was used in Hughes & Hutchins, 2011); General Elimination methodology, which seeks to identify and eliminate possible alternative explanations for causal attribution (Cook, Scriven, Coryn, & Evergreen, 2010); Contribution Analysis (Mayne, 2001); and Collaborative Outcomes Reporting (Dart, 2008; Dart & Roberts, 2014). All of these methods explicitly seek to provide justified claims around causality. Collaborative Outcomes Reporting may be particularly suited, as it is a participatory approach that may fit well within the ethos of programs such as Landcare.

Conclusion

Through the lens of evaluating the embedded facilitation in Landcare in Australia, we have identified four key challenge areas, with corresponding practices, for evaluating embedded facilitation generally.

Key recommended practices for evaluating embedded facilitation include mapping out the program theory and being ready to redefine it over time as the intervention changes. Clarifying the program theory serves two important purposes. First, it allows a locally shared understanding of the desired end-outcomes, and second, it enables the identification of interim outcomes that play an important role in establishing causal relationships between the facilitation and the outcomes of interest. To avoid engagement fatigue, we emphasize the importance of adopting evaluation approaches that engender ownership and minimize the time that evaluation consumes for communities. Effective approaches here include using participatory evaluation that is built into existing activities. To deal with the "unbounded" network aspects of embedded facilitation, we suggest approaches that are able to map and value connections between people (i.e., networks and social capital). To demonstrate the impact of embedded evaluation in a more rigorous manner, we recommend looking into some of the more in-depth qualitative and mixed-method impact approaches such as Process Tracing (as was used in Hughes & Hutchins, 2011), General Elimination methodology (Cook, Scriven, Coryn, & Evergreen, 2010), Contribution Analysis (Mayne, 2001), and Collaborative Outcomes Reporting (Dart, 2008; Dart & Roberts, 2014). All of these methods explicitly seek to provide justified claims around causality. Collaborative Outcomes Reporting may be particularly suited, as it fits well within the ethos of programs such as Landcare.

References

Ayers, J., Anderson, S., Pradhan, S., & Rossing, T. (2012). *Participatory monitoring, evaluation, reflection and learning for community-based adaptation: PMERL manual, a manual for local practitioners.* London: CARE International, International Institute for Environment and Development.

Bailey, M. (2006). Landcare: Myth or reality. In S. Lockie & F. Vanclay (Eds.), *Critical Landcare.* Key Paper Series No. 5 (pp. 129–142). Albury, Australia: Centre for Rural Social Research, Charles Sturt University.

Benjamin, L., & Greene, J. (2009). From program to network: The evaluator's role in today's public problem-solving environment. *American Journal of Evaluation, 30,* 296.

Campbell, A. (1989). Landcare in Australia: An overview. *Australian Journal of Soil and Water Conservation, 2,* 18–20.

Campbell, A. (2006). Facilitating landcare: Conceptual and practical dilemmas. In S. Lockie & F. Vanclay, (Eds.), (*Critical Landcare.* Key Paper Series No. 5 (pp. 143–152). Albury, Australia: Centre for Rural Social Research, Charles Sturt University.

Carson, L., Twyford, V., & Meek, T. (2005). Improving accountability for participatory processes through effective evaluation, Engaged systems: Evaluating engagement. Retrieved from http://www.engagingcommunities2005.org/abstracts/S116-carson-l.html

Colliver, R. (2011). Community-based governance in social-ecological systems: An inquiry into the marginalisation of Landcare in Victoria, Australia. (Doctor of Philosophy Thesis, Murdoch University). Available from core.kmi.open.ac.uk/download/pdf/11236988.pdf

Compton, E., & Beeton, R. (2012). An accidental outcome: Social capital and its implications for Landcare and the "status quo." *Journal of Rural Studies, 28,* 149–160.

Cook, T., Scriven, M., Coryn, C., & Evergreen, S. (2010). Contemporary thinking about causation in evaluation: A dialogue with Thomas Cook and Michael Scriven. *American Journal of Evaluation, 31*, 105–117.

Curtis, A., & De Lacy, T. (2006). Examining the assumptions underlying Landcare. In S. Lockie & F. Vanclay (Eds.), *Critical Landcare*. Key Paper Series No. 5 (pp. 185–200). Albury, Australia: Centre for Rural Social Research, Charles Sturt University.

Curtis, A., & Lockwood, M. (2000). Landcare and catchment management in Australia: Lessons for state-sponsored community participation. *Society & Natural Resources, 12*, 61–73.

Curtis, A., & Sample, R. (2010). *Community-based NRM in Victoria: Contributing to dialogue, learning and action*. Albury, Australia: Institute for Land, Water and Society, Charles Sturt University.

Curtis, A., Robertson, A., & Race, D. (1998). Lessons from recent evaluations of natural resource management programs in Australia. *Australian Journal of Environmental Management, 5*, 108–130.

Dart, J. (2008). *Report on outcomes and get everyone involved: The participatory performance story reporting technique*. Perth, Australia: Australasian Evaluation Society Conference.

Dart, J., & McGarry, P. (2006). People-focused program logic. Presented at the Australasian Evaluation Society Conference, Darwin, Australia.

Dart, J., & Roberts, M. (2014). Collaborative outcomes reporting. Retrieved from http://betterevaluation.org/plan/approach/cort

East Gippsland Catchment Management Authority. (2010). 2009/2010 Landcare performance story. Retrieved from http://eastgippsland.landcarevic.net.au/resources/regional-documentation/landcare-report-cards/PerformanceStory.pdf/view

Eriksson, L. (2012). *Knowledge translation in Vietnam: evaluating facilitation as a tool for improved neonatal health and survival*. (Doctoral Dissertation, Uppsala University). Available from *Digital Comprehensive Summaries of Uppsala Dissertations from the Faculty of Medicine, 785*, 59.

Ewing, S. (2006). "Small is beautiful": The place of the case study in Landcare Evaluation. In S. Lockie & F. Vanclay (Eds.), *Critical Landcare* (pp. 175–184). Albury, Australia: Centre for Rural Social Research, Charles Sturt University.

Fenton, M. (2007). *An evaluation of the national natural resource management facilitator network: Australian Government NRM facilitators*. Department of Environment and Heritage, Canberra.

Goulburn Broken Catchment Management Authority. (2010). *Landcare*. Retrieved from http://www.gbcma.vic.gov.au/downloads/Landcare/Report_Card_Landcare_Dl_front_back.pdf

Grant, A., & Curtis, A. (2004). Refining evaluation criteria for public participation using stakeholder perspectives of process and outcomes. *Rural Society, 14*, 142–162.

Hanna, K., Dale, A., & Ling, C. (2009). Social capital and quality of place: Reflections on growth and change in a small town. *Local Environment, 14*, 31–44.

Hassall & Associates. (2003). *Evaluation of the NHT Phase 1 facilitator, coordinator and community support networks*. Australia: Department of Environment and Heritage and Department of Agriculture Fisheries and Forestry.

Hogan, C. (2002). *Understanding facilitation, theory and principles*. London, UK: Kogan Page.

Hughes, K., & Hutchins, C. (2011). *Can we obtain the required rigor without experimentation? Oxfam GB's non-experimental global performance framework*. Retrieved from http://www.ipdet.org/files/publication-can_we_obtain_the_required_rigour_without_randomization.pdf

International Association of Facilitators. (2006). *The International Association of Facilitators handbook: Creating a culture of collaboration*. San Francisco, CA: Jossey-Bass.

Kaufman, S., Ozawa, C., & Shmueli, D. (2014). Evaluating participatory decision processes: Which methods inform reflective practice? *Evaluation and Program Planning*, 42, 11–20.

Lockie, S., & Vanclay, F. (Eds.). (2006). *Critical Landcare*. Key Paper Series No. 5. Albury, Australia: Centre for Rural Social Research, Charles Sturt University.

Mayne, J. (2001). Addressing attribution through contribution analysis: Using performance measures sensibly. *Canadian Journal of Program Evaluation*, 16, 1–24.

Otoo, S., Agapitova, N., & Behrens, J. (2009). The capacity development results framework: *A strategic and results-oriented approach to learning for capacity-development*. Retrieved from http://siteresources.worldbank.org/EXTCDRC/Resources/CDRF_Paper .pdf?resourceurlname=CDRF_Paper.pdf

Oxford English Dictionary. (2010). Oxford English Dictionary (3rd ed.). Oxford, UK: Oxford University Press.

Raetz, S. (2012, May). *Evaluation of the regional landcare facilitator program report. Department of Agriculture Fisheries and Forestry Australia and Clear Horizon Consulting*. Retrieved from http://www.daff.gov.au/__data/assets/pdf_file/0006/2255910 /daff-regional-landcare-facilitator-program-evaluation-report.pdf

Roberts, K. (1998). *Development of a coexistive evaluation model for Landcare Queensland*. Australia: Centre for Integrated Resource Management, University of Queensland.

Shadish, W., Cook, T., & Leviton, L. (1991). Foundations of program evaluation: *Theories of practice*. Oakland, CA: Sage.

Sobels, J., Curtis, A., & Lockie, S. (2001). The role of Landcare group networks in rural Australia: Exploring the contribution of social capital. *Journal of Rural Studies*, 7, 265–276.

Taylor, M., Plastrik, P., Coffman, J., & Whatley, A. (2014). *Part 2 of a guide to network evaluation, evaluating networks for social change: A case book*. Network Impact and Centre for Evaluation Innovation.

UNESCO. (2009). *On Target: A guide for monitoring and evaluating community based projects*. Paris, France: Author.

URS Australia. (2001). *Evaluation of investment in Landcare support projects*. Australia: Department of Agriculture, Fisheries and Forestry.

Walker, R. (1998). *The National Landcare Program: What has it changed? A compilation of evaluations of the National Landcare Program 1992–1998*. Natural Heritage Trust, Department of Agriculture, Fisheries and Forestry.

White, H., & Phillips, D. (2012). *Addressing attribution of cause and effect in small n impact evaluations: Towards an integrated framework*. Retrieved from http://www .3ieimpact.org/media/filer_public/2012/06/29/working_paper_15.pdf

JESSICA DART, PHD, *is the founder and Managing Director of Clear Horizon Consulting and holds a PhD in Evaluation.*

MEGAN ROBERTS *is a Researcher at Clear Horizon Consulting and holds a Graduate Certificate in Evaluation.*

INDEX